HORSES

An Owner's Guide

Diana Black

THUNDER BAY
P·R·E·S·S

First Published in 2001 by
Thunder Bay Press
An imprint of the
Advantage Publishers Group
5880 Oberlin Drive, San Diego,
CA 92121-4794

www.advantagebooksonline.com

All notations of errors or omissions should
by addressed to Thunder Bay Press, editorial
department, at the above address. All other
correspondence (author enquiries,
permissions) concerning the content of this
book should be addressed to Regency
House Publishing Limited, 3 Mill Lane,
Broxbourne, Hertfordshire, EN10 7AZ, UK.

ISBN 1-57145-570-1

Library of Congress Cataloging-in-Publication
Data available upon request.

Printed in China

1 2 3 4 5 6 00 01 02 03 04

**The publishers wish to stress most
emphatically that persons engaging in the
sport of riding must not do so without the
protection of officially approved headgear.**

All photographs are © **Peter Whittaker** other than
those on pages 4–5, 18, 19, 20, 22 below, 24, 25
top, 29, 42–43, 75, 76–77, 78, 98 below, 104–105,
114–115, 120–121, 123, 128, 132–133, 142 below,
143, 148–149, 164, 169, 180, 182, 184, 187, 188 left,
191, 197, 204–205, 210, 213, 215, 220 below, 222,
225–226, 227, 228, 232–233, 238, 242–243, 246–247,
248, 250–251 which are © **Kit Houghton** and
pages 12, 16 both, 17 below, 21, 25 below, 28 and
29 below, 38 below, 44, 45, 46, 48 all, 49, 56, 57,
58, 61, 64, 65, 79, 81, 82–83 all, 88 all below,
96–97, 101, 102, 107, 109, 112, 113, 122 below,
126–127, 135 all, 146–147, 166–167, 169 top, 172
both, 173, 189, 192, 194 left, 196 left, 198 above,
206–207, 235, 240–241, 245, 249 which are ©
Regency House Publishing Ltd.

Jacket
Front: © Kit Houghton. Insets: © Regency House
Publishing Ltd.
Back: © Regency House Publishing Ltd.

The author and photographer would like to thank
Claire Wardle, Debby Pumfrett, Lauren & Tonia
Hart, Sally, Hunter and Rebecca Diack, Catherine,
Hannah and Becky Rousell and Sue Abrahamson.

CONTENTS

INTRODUCTION

For centuries, the horse played a vital part in our lives. It was our only form of transport, used as a working animal on farms, in mining and in times of war.

Nowadays, riding is a popular leisure activity, one of the top five most popular sports, with livery yards and riding schools proliferating. Selective breeding has allowed the horse to develop into a supreme athlete, capable of incredible stamina and agility, with the result that more and more people have become interested in competing at high level in dressage, showjumping, eventing, showing and endurance events.

This great leap in popularity makes it all the more important that owners, potential owners and those entrusted with the care of horses should have a true understanding of every aspect of their management.

Nowadays, with ready-prepared feeds available and modern materials making tack lighter and more durable, looking after horses has become less of a chore; but it is still a complex, though rewarding subject. Much can be learned by simply observing your horse and noting his behaviour, reading up on the subject, and learning from your

own experience. Unless you are wealthy enough to be able to keep your horse at full livery, owning a horse will always be demanding of your time and energy and should be regarded as a way of life rather than a hobby. Remember that a strict routine should be maintained if a horse is to thrive.

This is a basic outline of the correct procedures, along with useful tips that will make your partnership with your horse mutually rewarding. Remember that a happy, healthy horse will willingly work for you, making riding and competing a pleasure for you both.

LEFT: Becoming a horse owner for the first time will make you realize just how much care and attention horses need, particularly throughout the harsher winter months.

OPPOSITE: Once a good relationship with your horse ihas been established you will be surprised to find how rewarding it is, especially when it comes to competing. As the rosettes start to arrive, all the hard work you have both put in will seem fully justified.

OVERLEAF: First ponies provide young children with a vital grounding in caring for horses as well as riding them.

Chapter One
CONFORMATION

When considering what kind of horse you would like, be it a Shetland pony or a Thoroughbred, it is important to understand the rules of conformation which apply to all breeds, as a horse that is well made is far less likely to become unsound.

From a distance, study the horse from all angles. He should stand square and the overall impression should be of balance, harmony and symmetry. The head should not be too large and should sit neatly on the neck, which should be gently arched, neither too long nor too short, tapering gradually to slightly sloping shoulders. The legs should be straight and clean with a generous amount of bone below the knee and well developed joints. Looking at the horse from behind, make sure that the hindlegs are level with the forelegs and that the quarters are even. The buttocks should be well developed and the tail set high, which is important for impulsion and speed. The chest should be broad and deep to accommodate good heart and lung function.

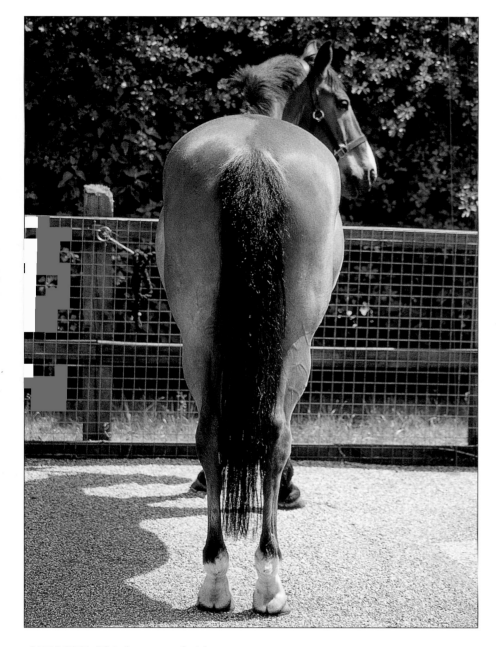

likely to be clumsy and therefore prone to injury.

The coat should be bright and glossy and should lie flat; it is a good indication of a horse's general health. Look carefully at the head. This should give an indication of the horse's character. The expression should be alert, kind and intelligent, with ears pricked forward and the eyes clear and bright. A rolling eye could be an indication of bad temper as well as pain. A 'pig eye', one in which there is a lot of white showing, is said to indicate obstinacy or wilfulness.

Remember, however, that there are exceptions to every rule: often the most unpromising turn out to be amazingly talented, proving that first impressions are not necessarily always correct.

COMMON DEFECTS

Legs These, along with the feet, take enormous amounts of punishment during a horse's lifetime. He needs correctly shaped legs if they are not to be susceptible to lameness and to maintain a good action. The knees of the forelegs are important for

OPPOSITE: This horse and rider appear in perfect harmony as they work in the manège. However, the rider is perhaps a little too large for her pony.

ABOVE: Always check the horse from all angles, looking for symmetry. If one side is more developed than the other, a long-term weakness could be indicated.

RIGHT: Pay particular attention to the horse's legs, looking for comformation defects as well as for wear and tear.

TAKING A CLOSER LOOK

Now approach the horse. Examine each leg in turn, checking that they are perfectly straight and that the hooves are symmetrical with plenty of heel. Make sure they match the size of the horse. (A large horse with small feet will have problems with weight distribution, when undue pressure will be put on the delicate bones of the foot which could, in turn, lead to foot disease and lameness.) Likewise, a small horse with proportionately large feet is

good balance: if, for example, the horse is 'over at the knee' or 'back at the knee', the weight will be unevenly distributed, causing extra strain on localized areas such as the heel. Toes turning in or out can cause strain on the pastern, fetlock and foot. The same rules apply to the hindlegs; hocks which are tucked under the buttocks or which are too far out from the body will hamper propulsion. Cow hocks and bowed hocks are also a sign of weakness and would render the horse undesirable.

The Back This is subject to enormous strain because it has to carry the weight of a rider; it is vital, therefore, that it is as strong as possible. Look for well developed muscles, as they are the major support of the back. The horse's natural conformation is also an important factor: horses with long backs are more likely to suffer from strain and sway (hollow) backs, another feature of long-backed horses, is another sign of weakness. Horses with short backs have an advantage in that they are usually strong and often agile; however they can be prone to overreaching. It is also difficult to fit a saddle to them and the rider may end up sitting nearer the horse's loins, which is the weakest part of the back.

The Head and Neck A large head is a disadvantage in the field of competition, particularly in dressage and showing. The horse may have difficulty keeping his head in balance, and may find it impossible to hold it in an unsupported outline. A 'ewe neck' is when the top muscle is weaker than the bottom, giving the neck the appearance of being on upside-down: horses with this defect should be avoided as it is often impossible to correct. Likewise a bull neck should also be avoided as the horse will be difficult to control and it will be difficult to obtain sufficient flexion when schooling.

ABOVE: Look for a head and neck that is well set on the body. The head should be neither too small nor too large. Look for a kind eye and a happy disposition.

RIGHT: Even though many ponies seem to differ from horses, the same rules of conformation apply.

Chapter Two
BREEDS, TYPES, COLOURS & MARKINGS

BREEDS AND TYPES

Horses and ponies belong to one of two specific groups. A **breed** consists of horses and ponies which are genetically similar and which have been selectively bred to produce consistent characteristics, while reinforcing their best features; they are recognized as such in official stud books. They fall into four distinct categories: hotbloods, warmbloods, coldbloods and ponies.

Hotbloods are highly strung and include the Thoroughbred and Arab. They have been bred for their enormous stamina and speed, evident when racing in which they excel.

Warmbloods are calmer creatures, having a heavier build than hotbloods. They have been bred for their extravagant paces and biddable natures; they are excellent performers in jumping and dressage. They are the result of interbreeding with heavier coldbloods such as Shires and Cleveland Bays and were originally bred as warhorses and for lighter work on farms, mainly in northern Europe. Examples are the Hanoverian, Dutch Warm Blood and Holstein.

Coldbloods, as mentioned above, are the heavier types of horse such as the Irish Draught and Percheron. They are less common nowadays, heavy horses on farms being a thing of the past, and are now more commonly seen in the show ring.

Finally, there is the pony, which covers all the native breeds measuring under 14.2hh.

A **type**, however, is the result of crossing breeds to produce a specific kind of horse intended for a specific purposes, such as the cob and the hunter.

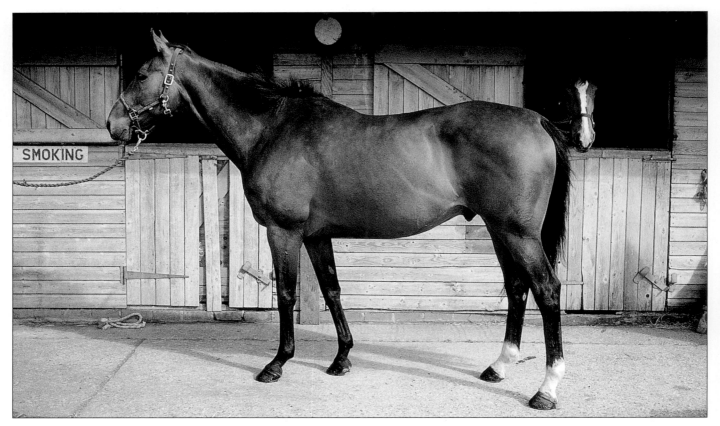

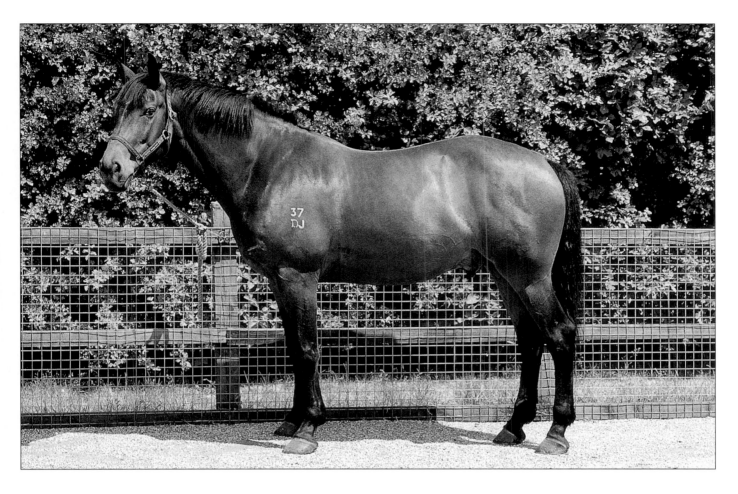

ABOVE: Warmbloods are known for their calm temperaments and extravagant paces. They often excel in jumping and dressage.

LEFT: Cobs are workmanlike, strong and dependable. They are suitable for any member of the family.

OPPOSITE: The Thoroughbred has been developed for speed and stamina, hence the long limbs and deep chest.

OVERLEAF: The hunter is a type originally meant for the hunting field, although more recently they have been used for general riding and showing.

17

COLOURS

The wild horses which originally roamed the planet would have been a dull muddy colour, allowing them to blend into their surroundings. Nowadays, through selective breeding, horses come in a variety of colours and markings.

Breeding a horse to be a certain colour is an extremely complicated business and is achieved by mixing various genetic material. This is a tricky process as some colour genes also have an effect on temperament and performance. For example, the old saying that chestnuts have a fiery nature often seems to be correct. Racehorse breeders tend to favour horses carrying the black gene, present in the bay, and they do seem predominant among the winners.

In the US and Australia, particularly, selective breeding to produce unusual colours has become quite common, and horses now come in a striking variety of colours and markings. However, most horses fit into the basic categories listed in this section.

BELOW: Colour is determined by genetics, and therefore some colours can be more pronounced in different breeds. These wild horses carry a variety of colours in their gene pool.

OPPOSITE
ABOVE: Bay.
BELOW: Chestnut.

Bay This is probably the most common colour, the coat varying from a light reddish-brown to deep black-brown with black on the lower legs, muzzle and the tips of the ears, the mane and tail being also black. Bays are a genetically modified form of black. Despite its popularity, only one actual breed has emerged – the Cleveland Bay.

Brown The coat consists of shades of nearly black or brown, which are spread evenly over the body except for the areas around the eyes, the girth, muzzle and flanks, which have a lighter 'mealy' appearance. The mane and tail may be liver, reddish-brown or nearly-black.

Chestnut This is a red coat of any shade, ranging from a light to a dark reddish-brown which is known as liver chestnut. The mane and tail are usually of a similar colour or may be flaxen (these are called sorrels). Non-chestnut parents may have chestnut foals; if both parents are chestnut they will always have progeny that are this colour.

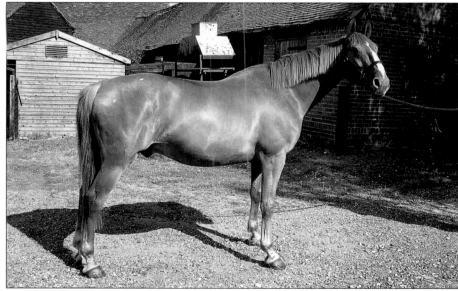

Dun There are four variations on the colour known as dun, which can have red, yellow, mouse and blue tinges. Dun horses have darker markings on the muzzle and legs with the addition of a dorsal stripe which may be black or brown. Several breeds of this colour type have been developed, the most common being the Fjord.

Grey Technically, this is not a colour but a pattern superimposed over other colours. Greys are born with dark skin which progressively lightens with age, leading to most of them eventually turning white in varying degrees. This is not necessarily a sign of old age and is known as greying out. They come with two different coat patterns, the favourite being dappled grey which is the result of the lightening of the coat usually of a horse which is born dark grey, known as iron or blue-grey. As the horse's colour fades, the dappling remains mainly on the legs. The other type is known as flea-bitten; these greys never turn completely white, but seem to revert instead to the base colour they had at birth: for example, some may develop blue, black or red speckles; moreover, injuries such as bites and cuts will also grow over in that colour.

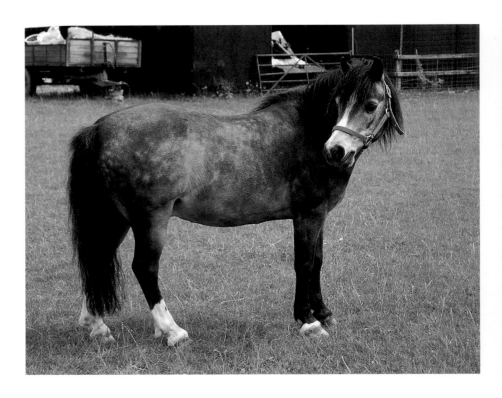

ABOVE: Dun.

RIGHT: Dapple Grey.

Black There are two types: non-fading black, which only fades under extreme conditions, the overall effect being a coat of a metallic, iridescent or bluish shine. When combined with white markings, such as a star or socks, it is particularly striking. Fading black is probably a more common variation: the black colour will only be retained if the horse is kept stabled or rugged when exposed to the elements.

There may also be fading through sweating, when lighter patches are left under the saddle and girth areas. When the summer coat comes through, the coat will have a black sheen, but never the blue metallic effect of the non-fading type, and during the season will become a reddish-brown in appearance. Black horses aren't popular in very hot climates such as the Australian Outback, as black absorbs heat, leading to

skin irritation. Breeds selectively bred for their black colour tend to appear in colder climates, for example, the Fell, Friesian and Canadian horse.

ABOVE: True black horses are rare as most tend to fade in summer to dark-brown.

Cremello Sometimes known as pseudo-albinos, these horses have cream-coloured coats which are slightly darker then any white markings present. The eyes are pale blue and glassy in appearance. This colour is not popular, particularly in hot climates, where strong sunlight can be irritating to light-coloured eyes. Such horses are also more prone to skin cancers and chafing. However, in cooler climates they can do rather well and their striking appearance is unusual.

Spotted Spotting can occur in many breeds but is most common in the Appaloosa; in fact, the breed has given its name to the spotted pattern. Markings vary from coloured spots on white, white spots on colour, or a scattering of small white or coloured spots.

Palomino Much prized, these horses have beautiful golden coats ranging from pale to dusky tan; they are usually the result of a cremello crossed with a chestnut. However, the breeding of palominos is a complicated business and is more common in the US where the colour originated. Ideally, the mane and tail should be pure white.

Roan This comes in a variety of colours and is composed of a pattern of white hairs over a base colour which is only confined to the body, the head and legs remaining in the base colour. Unlike greys, the colour does not fade, but any nicks or scratches will grow back covered in the base colour. They come in three basic types: strawberry roan, which has a chestnut base coat, blue roan which has black, and red roan which has bay. The mane, tail, legs and muzzle markings will be the same colour as the base coat.

ABOVE: Spotted.

CENTRE: Palomino.

RIGHT: Strawberry Roan.

OPPOSITE: Cremello.

Coloured The definition of a coloured horse is any colour combined with white. In the US, these are known as pintos; however, there is a huge variety of colours and markings with varying degrees of white and colour which have different names. They are highly prized and their appearance is extremely striking. In the UK, coloured types are less prized and tend to be predominately ponies: however, horses of the type are now becoming more popular. Varieties are skewbald, which are any having colour patches with white, and piebald, which is black-and-white.

Coloured horses are gaining in popularity and it is now commonplace to see them in professional showjumping circuits and in the dressage arena.

Blaze

Star

Some horses have more pronounced markings than others. They are a good means of identification as they remain with the horse throughout its lifetime.

OPPOSITE: This hunter has a striking star marking.

Star and Snip

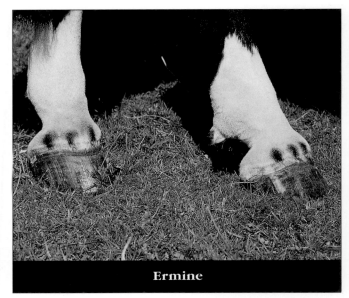

Ermine

Socks

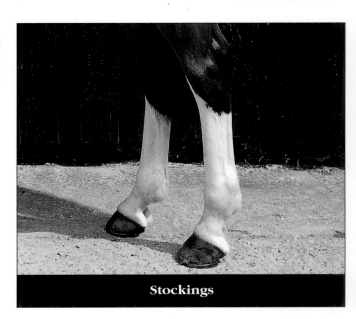

Stockings

Chapter Three
CHOOSING A HORSE

This book is largely concerned with looking after horses and riding them; but as most readers are potential owners, it is useful to know how to go about choosing one.

Before even considering a horse of your own you must ask yourself some serious questions. Horses are not only demanding of your time but are also a drain on the pocket. It is assumed that you are already proficient in the saddle and have a basic knowledge of what is involved. But remember that it is foolhardy and potentially cruel to buy a horse before you have considered the following guidelines.

BELOW: Always look for a kind temperament, particularly if children are involved.

OPPOSITE: Make sure that any horse you buy fits your ability. Choose a steadier horse if you are inexperienced. These two seem to be quite happy together.

COST

Be aware that keeping a horse is a costly business: the initial cost of buying an animal is only the tip of the iceberg and you will need to make allowances for feed, shoeing, equipment, veterinary bills and insurance. You must also decide where and how your horse is to be kept. Some may be lucky enough to have their own accommodation; however, the majority of us have to keep our horses at livery, which ranges from the less expensive DIY arrangement, where you do most of the work yourself and pay for stabling and grazing, to total care – but at a price.

TIME

The amount of time you have or are prepared to devote to your horse is an important factor. Horses thrive on routine and become easily upset when this is disturbed. You will need to decide if you can adequately look after your horse yourself; alternatively, if you are a busy person, you may prefer a full livery service to give you more time to ride. But remember that full, or even part, livery does not come cheap: make sure that you can afford this as a regular expense.

ABILITY

As mentioned previously, you should never consider buying a horse until you are a proficient rider. First take a course of riding lessons and, if possible, ask the establishment owner if you can look after one of their horses to gain experience. Take advice from experienced equestrians and ask their opinion on as many aspects of the subject as you can. It may

be possible to keep your horse at the same establishment where you learned to ride, in which case others will be happy to keep an eye on you and offer useful tips. Always remember, however, that a horse that is suitable for you now may not be in a year or two's time, so you will have to take this into account.

REQUIREMENTS

When you are sure you have satisfied all the above criteria, you will need to think about the type of horse you wish to own. You should consider your own ability, size, shape and how much money you have to spend. The majority of potential horse owners have been riding for many years and have a good deal of experience: they may wish to develop their chosen field, perhaps dressage or showjumping and may require a better bred, younger and more athletic horse. These types of horse, usually Thoroughbreds or Warmbloods, tend to be expensive and will require quite a large financial outlay. For those with limited experience, however, there is an enormous range of horses from which to choose, many of them quite inexpensive. However, you must choose a

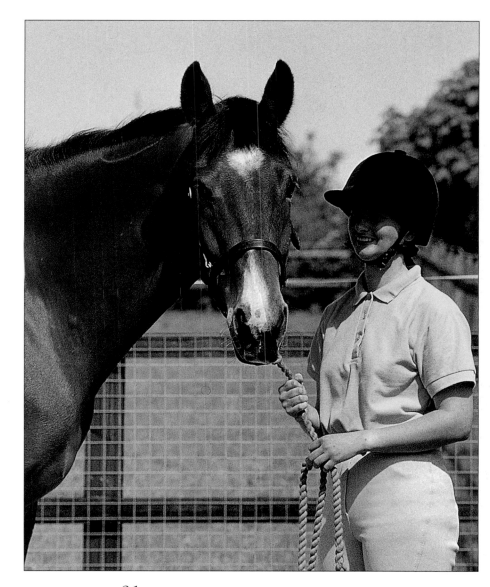

31

OPPOSITE and ABOVE: There are many tests for general soundness, and having a horse walked towards you and then away is just one of them. This should also be done in trot which may reveal further problems connected with the horse's action.

horse to fit your needs. For example, there is no point in buying a 14.2hh pony if you are 6-ft (1.83-m) tall, or a lively flashy horse if you have limited experience. Be sensible: choose a horse with a kind disposition, steady temperament and strong constitution and you can look forward to a happy, largely trouble-free relationship. If in any doubt, ask the advice of an experienced person.

WHERE TO LOOK

Remember that you are buying a living animal which could have any kind of history: it may be from a genuine loving home, or have been subjected to abuse. Be aware of the pitfalls as you are spending a not inconsiderable amount of money and there are unscrupulous people, trading in the horse world, who can be economical with the truth. Always take a knowledgeable person with you and don't allow yourself to be bullied or forced to succumb to a hard-luck story Where possible, steer clear of dealers unless they have been recommended; even if they have a good reputation they are unlikely to know the full history of the horse, and their fees can come expensive. There are plenty of other places to look, and maybe you should start closer to home. Your local riding school or stable yard may be able to sell you a horse, one you may already know well. Look at notice boards in saddlers or ask an experienced person if they know of any suitable horses for sale. The rule

ABOVE: Teenagers and young riders should try to find a horse that is experienced and reliable. Inexperienced young riders should never be tempted to buy a young or spirited animal.

OPPOSITE: Check the horse all over for possible defects.

of thumb is to stick to private sales where you are more likely to get an accurate past history; you will also see the horse in its home environment, which will give an inkling of the kind of life it has led so far. Avoid horse sales: they are only for the very experienced.

WHAT TO LOOK FOR

Once you find a horse that you like and which is suitable to your requirements, ask the owner as many questions as possible to establish the horse's history. It is a good idea to prepare a list of questions beforehand, such as: does the horse suffer from any ailments?, does it have any stable vices?, does it have any allergies?, how does it react to traffic? You can learn a good deal by doing your own detective work. First ask to see the horse in his stable; check that he seems happy and relaxed in his surroundings. Watch him moving around: a horse continually resting one leg may be lame. Should he have vices, he may reveal them now; does he crib-bite, weave or wind-suck? These are not good signs and the horse should no longer be considered. Look at where he sleeps; if he is on special bedding he may be suffering from allergies. Ask what he eats; specially prepared hay may also be an adverse indication, though many owners prefer to keep their animals on dust-free bedding and hay as a preventative measure.

Give him a pat and make his acquaintance. Are his ears forward and does he seem relaxed in your company; flattened ears and attempts to bite are a sign of an aggressive or territorial nature. Once you are happy with his stable manners, ask the owner to lead him out of the stable.

Satisfy yourself that his general appearance seems correct, following the guidelines in Chapter One. Then thoroughly look him over, noting any old injuries, particularly on the legs, and making sure that the tendons are hard and that the limbs are straight. Ask the owner to trot him up (you are now looking for signs of lameness); look at his head; does it dip up and down as he trots (this is usually a sign that he has pain in his legs or back). Watch him trotting from the front and from behind; he should be moving straight with an even, springy gait. You can also look at his teeth. It is possible to make a rough guess of his age by the length of the teeth and the amount of wear; however, your vet will be able to assess this more accurately; but you can make sure that his teeth meet, as overshot top teeth, known as 'parrot mouth', will classify him as

unsound. With this condition the horse may have difficulty cropping grass which could result in failure to gain weight or cause digestive problems.

TRYING HIM OUT

Before even attempting to mount an animal you do not know, practise safety by following this advice; this will also provide you with clues as to the horse's general well-being.

Watch carefully as he is being tacked up. Does he accept the bit freely; any reluctance could indicate a dental problem, or wilfulness. What type of bit is he ridden in? A severe bit could indicate that he is a bit of a handful. Watch carefully as he is being saddled up; does he lift his head up sharply as the saddle is placed on his back? This could indicate a sore back, likewise when the girth is being done up. Check the numnah: a thick one could also be a clue that he has a sensitive back.

Now ask the owner to ride the horse first, not only for your own safety but to see how the horse moves. It is obvious that he will go better for his owner, but you will be able to get an idea of his potential. Ask to see him walk, trot and canter and observe him over a few small jumps. If you are happy with his way of going and you are an experienced rider, you may try him out for yourself, putting him through his paces and, if possible, over a couple of jumps. By now, you should know if he is the horse for you. However, you will need to see how he reacts in traffic. Ask the owner to ride him out alongside a busy road and watch his reaction;

he should show no fear or panic. If you are happy with this you may wish to ride him out yourself, but you should only attempt this if accompanied by the owner.

In some cases, the owner may let you take the horse for a trial period, usually 1–2 weeks. This is an excellent idea: it not only gives you time to be sure that you want this horse, it also proves that the owner is genuine. Always ask if you can do this before committing to a sale.

VETTING

Now that all of these stages have been completed, you should feel confident in your choice. It is now time to get a vet involved. If you are buying locally, ask a reliable person to recommend one to you. If the horse is stabled far away you will need to commission a vet in that area; don't be tempted to use the owner's vet, he may be biased.

Vetting is expensive but is money well spent, not only for peace of mind, but also as an important part of the buying process. It can identify problems before the purchase, but is an important factor when it comes to insurance. Most insurance companies will not issue a certificate without a veterinary report. Make sure that you are present at the vetting, as the vet may wish to discuss relevant points with you.

THE PROCEDURE

The vet will usually begin by examining the horse in his stable. He will check the heart, lungs and sight and will also look at the teeth to gauge his age. (This can only be done with any certainty

up to the age of 8, after which time it will be an estimate.) The vet will also check for problems which may affect the horse's ability to eat. He will then feel him all over, checking for lumps, old injuries, particularly to the legs. The horse may display stable vices such as weaving, crib-biting and wind-sucking, which will all render him unsound.

Once satisfied, the vet will ask to see the horse trotted up on a hard surface; he will check that he is moving straight with no sign of lameness and has good flexion in all his limbs. He will also make a thorough examination of the hooves, checking that they are correctly balanced, and that the foot shows no evidence of disease.

He will then ask to see the horse ridden by its owner in all the gaits ending with a gallop. He will listen to the heart and lungs before and after exercise, which will reveal any problems; the hard exercise will also reveal lameness.

The horse will need to satisfy all these criteria before he can be pronounced fit and a certificate issued. You may wish to have further tests, such as x-rays to test for bone disease such as arthritis and navicular syndrome, or blood tests which will reveal if the horse is on drugs such as painkillers or sedatives to alter his temperament. These latter tests are not compulsory and will be a further source of expense; but they are well worth while to ensure peace of mind.

OPPOSITE: This rider has found a horse which is the right size and age. However, a trial period is recommended before purchase.

LOANING A HORSE

If you are not quite ready to commit yourself to a horse of your own, or are simply not confident enough to cope with all the above procedures, having a horse on loan may be a good option. If you look in your local newspaper or on the notice board in your saddler's you will usually see details of horses offered on full or shared loan. Often the owner is short of time or money, but does not wish to give up their horse entirely. Some owners will allow you to stable the horse in a yard of your choice, others may wish the horse to remain where it is. It could be – and this is ideal – that you already know the horse.

If this option appeals to you, make sure that you check the horse over thoroughly and find out as much as possible concerning his history. Take care to check out the guidelines before you start, including the periods when the horse will be in your sole charge, together with the financial commitment. A written contract, which both parties must sign, is also a good idea. It is a happy thought that many people who initially have a horse out on loan often end up buying and keeping it.

Chapter Four
THE HEALTHY HORSE

Keeping a horse healthy isn't exactly rocket science: it is a matter of getting the balance between feeding, exercise and good stable management right, as well as vigilance and the ability to recognize when something is wrong. Much of this comes down to experience, which you will gain in your day-to-day contact with your horse. However, there are rules which must be followed if he is to lead a happy and healthy life. These are outlined in the chapters on stable management, feeding, and fitness, all of which are vital to your horse's well-being.

This chapter explains how to prevent certain diseases from occurring and how to recognize the signs of ill health. A runny nose or eyes could well be a symptom of something more serious, so follow these guidelines, and remember to call the vet if you have any worries or doubts.

BELOW: A healthy animal should be happy, alert and remain full of vitality all year round.

OPPOSITE: Out for a ride: this pair are enjoying a pleasant day in the countryside.

DAILY HEALTH CHECK

Grooming presents a good opportunity for checking your horse over for sickness or injury. Tie him up and stand well back to look at the overall picture: firstly, does he look happy? Ideally he will be standing there, quite relaxed, perhaps resting one leg. Wake him up and get him to stand square. He should be able to do this easily, but if he persists in resting a leg this could be a sign of injury. Check that his eyes are bright and shining and free of discharge, likewise his nose. Look at his flanks: in a relaxed state, his breathing should be barely perceptible.

Now start to groom him, following behind with your other hand to check for lumps or abrasions, working your way down each leg in turn to check for puffiness. This could indicate a strain or injury caused by a kick from another horse in the field. Also examine the skin: it should appear clean with no raw patches indicative of skin disease or a rub from a piece of tack. Pick out the feet at least twice a day or as often as necessary, checking that there is no damage such as puncture wounds, bruising from stones, or signs of disease of the frog, such as thrush, foot rot, or sore spots caused by overreaching. Finally, give him a quick trot up to check for lameness.

ABOVE: Find time, preferably twice a day, to look your horse over for signs of injury or disease.

OPPOSITE: In good weather, horses are at their happiest and healthiest when out at grass. However, make sure that the horse's weight is carefully monitored and that he is not prone to laminitis (see pages 57–58).

OVERLEAF: Horses at grass can exercise as they please. As this is also a time when accidents can occur, make sure they are regularly checked over for injury and that shoes have not worked themselves loose.

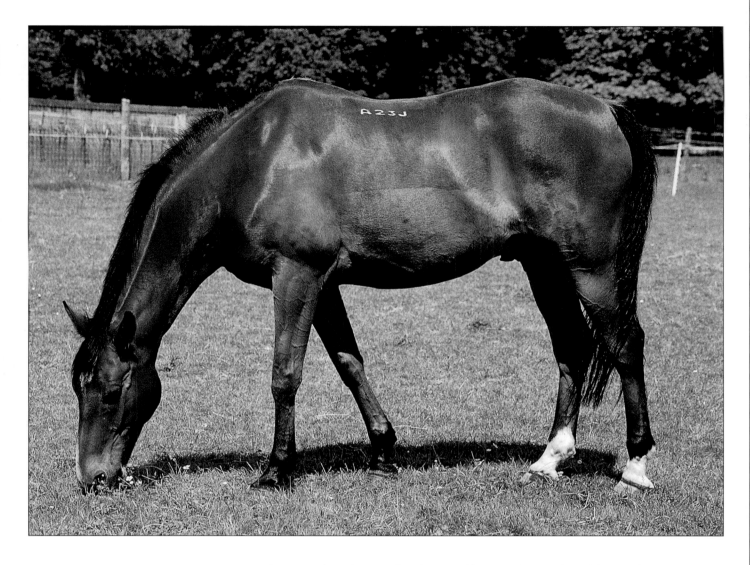

PREVENTIVE MEDICINE

Like us, horses are subject to many diseases: however, maintaining them in good health will reduce the risk of more serious conditions. Many opportunist diseases affect either the very young, the elderly, or horses in a poor neglected state. Tetanus and equine influenza may be contracted by any horse and are potentially lethal, so it is vital that there is yearly vaccination against them. Horses are also susceptible to worms which they pick up while grazing, which if left untreated can seriously undermine their constitution and even cause death. To avoid this, a regular worming programme must be introduced: your local vet will be able to advise you regarding treatment, but the general procedure is to worm every 6 weeks and more often at certain times of year. Wormers come in powders which can be mixed into feed; some horses will happily eat this, others may reject the strange taste. Although they are easy to administer, you must watch when they are consumed to make sure that the required dose has been taken. The other type is a paste which comes in a syringe: this is rather more problematical as it has to be inserted into the horse's mouth and discharged very quickly before he gets the taste of it and spits it out; a bowl of feed close at hand has to be eaten afterwards to ensure that it all goes down.

Another way of preventing disease is regular shoeing, which is necessary every 4–6 weeks depending on how quickly the feet grow. It is tempting to neglect this as the process is expensive; but feet left to grow too long can cause enormous problems, resulting in navicular syndrome, laminitis and tendon injury.

Make sure that teeth are checked for any rough areas of growth which may cause discomfort, and which may require rasping down so that the horse can continue to chew properly.

41

SIGNS OF ILLNESS

An important part of horse ownership is being able to recognize when your horse is unwell. This becomes easier with experience and as you get to know him. Many know instinctively when their horse is ailing when others can see nothing wrong at all. At the first inkling of a problem, watch him carefully. Any of the symptoms listed below could be an indication of serious illness, such as colic, respiratory problems or an injury. First of all, try to ascertain if the symptoms are caused by external damage such as a strain or a kick, then call the vet.

- Sweating
- Rolling of the eyes
- Discharge from eyes and/or nose
- Heavy breathing
- Tucking-in at the flanks
- Looking towards or pecking at the stomach
- Excessive rolling
- Inability to move without pain
- A dejected look
- Loose or no motions
- Reluctance to stand on all four legs

THE VITAL SIGNS

Learning to recognize you horse's normal breathing pattern is important and will alert you to any abnormalities. At rest, a horse's respiration is 8–16 breaths per minute, a breath being one movement in and out. The breathing should not be clearly defined but can by felt by placing your hand on the ribcage. Rapid and obvious movement is a sure indication that the horse is stressed, either from internal pain or external injury, which is likely to be accompanied by a dejected look. If, however, he is alert and agitated, he may merely be reacting to something he can either hear or see in the distance.

TAKING THE TEMPERATURE

A veterinary thermometer is an important part of the first-aid kit. Read the instructions before using. Give the thermometer a good shake down and apply a little petroleum jelly. Standing to the side of the horse's rear, gently lift the tail to one side and insert the thermometer, holding it against the wall of the rectum. Hold it in place for the prescribed amount of time. A horse's normal temperature should be 37.5–38°C (99.5–100.4°F). A rise of a degree or more should be taken seriously.

CHECKING THE PULSE

The pulse is strong and can be taken at various sites, i.e. behind the pastern, either side of the fetlock, where it is known as the digital pulse, or you may use a stethoscope behind the elbow. However, the easiest and most convenient place to take the pulse is where the artery crosses the

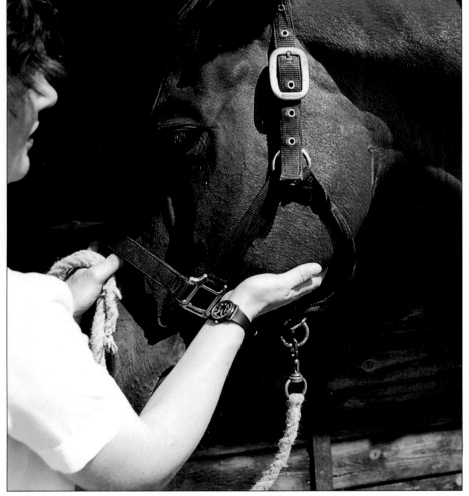

OPPOSITE: Checking the pulse.

BELOW: This Anglo-Arab is in the peak of condition and enjoying his exercise period.

inside of the jawbone. Remember to use your fingers only as your thumb has a strong pulse of its own. At rest, the normal pulse rate is 36–40 beats per minute.

Increased pulse and respiration when at rest may indicate that the horse is suffering, due to pain or illness, stress or excitement.

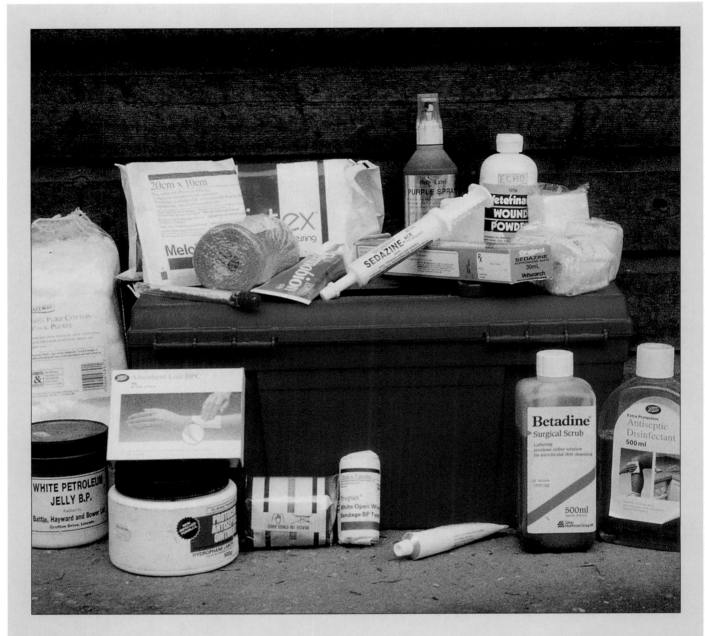

First Aid

All horse owners should have a comprehensive first-aid kit, which should be kept in an airtight container and placed where anyone can easily locate it. A second kit is advisable for when the horse is away from home, i.e. at competitions.

ABOVE: A well equipped first-aid kit.

First-Aid Kit

- Large roll of cotton wool
- 3–4 rolls of gamgee
- 3–4 rolls of crêpe/self-adhesive bandage
- 3-4 wound dressings (non-stick)
- Poultices (for inflamed puncture wounds)
- Poultice boot or tape to hold a dressing in position
- Wound powder/antiseptic cream or spray
- Salt
- Liquid antiseptic or iodine-based scrub
- Anti-inflammatory analgesic sachets (on vet's advice only)
- Elastic support bandages for joints
- Surgical tape
- Tweezers
- Blunt-ended scissors
- Veterinary thermometer
- A clean bowl
- A torch

SIMPLE FLESH WOUNDS

Horses are prone to infections, so once a wound has been identified, act quickly. Most flesh wounds can be treated at home. Flush out the wound with clean water, removing all dirt and debris. Next boil up some water, let it cool slightly and add either salt or an iodine-based scrub. Dip a ball of cotton wool into the solution and give the wound a thorough clean – be as thorough as the horse will allow. Repeat until you are confident that the wound is clean. Using more cotton wool, dry the wound and apply some antiseptic. If not too serious, let the air get to the wound, which will aid the healing process; if more serious, apply a dressing. If in any doubt, or if the wound becomes inflamed or has a foul-smelling discharge, call the vet.

wounds which are adjacent to or on a joint will require urgent veterinary attention, as infection could easily spread to the joint causing irreparable damage.

Likewise puncture wounds, which can be very deep, concealing internal damage. As with all wounds, the most important thing is to get them as clean as

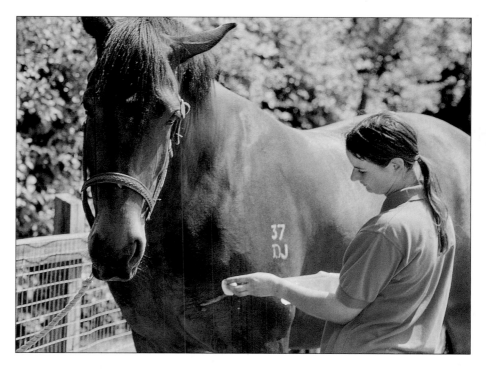

possible, using clean fresh water; don't apply any treatments until the vet sees them. If bleeding is excessive, plug the wound with cotton wool and hold it in position with a bandage to stem the flow. Call the vet urgently: he may apply sutures and prescribe antibiotics to combat infection.

ABOVE: Wounds should be cleaned meticulously, using a sterilized bowl with boiled water, cotton wool and antiseptic.

LEFT (BOTH): Correct bandaging takes skill and experience, and the novice handler should seek advice. The hock is one of the most difficult areas to bandage and care must be taken that it is done not too tightly and that there are no pressure points. Do not bandage over the point of the hock.

SERIOUS WOUNDS

It is usually quite obvious when a wound is serious; it may have blood pouring from it, or there may be a large gash or tear which will require veterinary attention and sutures. Other wounds may appear superficial, but could in fact be potentially serious. All

Chapter Five
AILMENTS & DISORDERS

Like us, horses are subject to disease and injury. Checking them daily, ideally when grooming, is a good way of spotting when something is wrong, when it can be dealt with immediately before it becomes more serious.

LEG DISORDERS AND LAMENESS
Most of the disorders you are likely to encounter are centred around the leg and hoof, and usually cause lameness. When one considers how fine and slender a horse's legs are, it is surprising the amount of weight they are expected to carry, not only his own enormous body weight but that of a rider as well. During exercise, the bones and tendons are subjected to huge amounts of pressure, with strains of the ligaments and tendons a common result. Horses can also be quite clumsy and seemingly unaware of the potential damage a metal shoe can inflict. Self-inflicted wounds, such as overreaching and bruising of the bulb of the heel, are also common and cause damage resulting in severe lameness.

A little common sense can eliminate many of these injuries. Don't work an unfit horse too hard: begin with gentle exercise and build up gradually to strengthen muscles and tendons. Damage can be avoided by using protective equipment when exercising, such as tendon boots, overreach boots and brushing boots, all of which can protect the horse from a lower leg-strike injury. Avoid trotting on roads for prolonged periods; concussion can cause tendon injury as well as foot disease such as navicular syndrome.

A large percentage of lameness stems from the foot. Nowadays, because horses have the protection of shoes, the sole remains relatively soft, leaving it vulnerable to puncture wounds and bruising. If left untreated

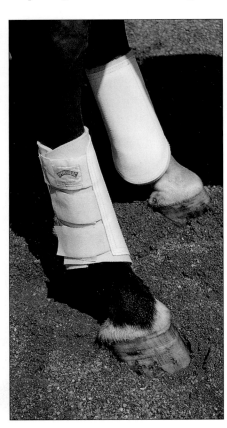

Horses are very susceptible to leg injuries; consequently, there are many kinds of protective boots available. Brushing boots (FAR LEFT) protect the lower leg from a strike from the opposite leg. Knee boots (LEFT) protect the knees should a horse fall on to a hard surface.

OPPOSITE: This horse is wearing brushing boots during its schooling session over jumps.

these can lead to a build-up of infection under the sole which causes excruciating pain. Be careful when riding over uneven ground, particularly in flinty or stony areas.

Broken Knee Despite its name, this is not a fracture but is when the skin of the knee is broken due to a stumble when the horse lands on his knees. If your horse is prone to stumbling, make sure knee boots are fitted for protection before riding out, also if you are riding in slippery conditions.

SELF-INFLICTED INJURIES
These are troublesome, often causing prolonged lameness. They occur when the horse strikes one leg against the other. Prevention by protection is the best way of avoiding these injuries.

Overreaching This is the most common self-inflicted injury and occurs when the horse strikes the heel or pastern of the foreleg with the hind. Because the horse is shod, the damage can be considerable; in severe cases a tendon may be severed or a bone

This horse is well protected for riding cross-country. He is wearing exercise bandages and overreach boots on his forelegs and leather brushing boots on the hind.

broken. At the very least it can cause a nasty laceration which, because of its situation, can take a very long time to heal and is very painful. This type of injury is common in horses which have short backs and in young unbalanced horses. Overreach and tendon boots protect against this type of injury. For horses which constantly suffer this type of injury, it is a good idea to also use turn-out boots, but be careful; wearing boots for prolonged periods can damage the skin of the legs.

Brushing Another injury occurring mainly during exercise, caused when a leg strikes an opposite leg. This is common in horses which are narrow between the legs and also young unbalanced horses. Brushing boots are the best protection from this injury. Use these also when schooling, as tight turns and circles can contribute to this type of injury.

Treads These commonly occur when travelling and are injuries caused by a horse treading on the coronet, the ring of bone above

LEFT: Clarendon boots offer all-round protection during exercise. They are designed to protect from brushes and strikes from a hind foot on to a foreleg and, like most modern boots, are machine-washable.

OVERLEAF: Horses living at grass are closer to natural conditions than those which are stabled, as they can exercise and rest at will. However, left to their own devices they can still develop problems, so should be carefully monitored.

the hoof; risk of this can be reduced by bandaging right to the bottom of the coronet. Overreach boots can also be worn on all four feet to further protect the coronet band during a journey.

Tendon Injuries
Horses have very fine, slim legs in relation to their heavy bodies. During exercise, especially, an enormous amount of strain it put on the bones, ligaments and particularly the tendons of the lower leg. Tendon injuries can be avoided by not overworking an unfit horse and by not pushing a horse beyond its natural capabilities. Tendon injuries are common among racehorses, particularly jumpers, which are often pushed to extremes.

The first sign of a strain is usually lameness, the severity of pain depending on the level of injury. The horse may find it difficult to put his foot down and the injured area will feel hot and swollen. Injuries of this nature should never be ignored, and the first 48 hours are critical. First call the vet, who will recommend hosing the injured area with water for as long as possible to bring the swelling down and cool the area, as continued heat will cause further breakdown. The injured leg should then be strapped up in a support bandage, also the opposite good one, which will be taking the extra strain.

The horse will require box rest until he appears sound, when he should be returned to work slowly, with regular checks for further swelling or pain. If this occurs, continue treatment. More severe injuries, referred to as 'breakdowns', usually occur when

the injured tendon has been ignored or the horse has been put to work too soon. Old chronic injuries will result in permanently thickened or bowed tendons caused by a build-up of scar tissue. These are usually the result of either one bad injury or a build-up of several neglected slight strains.

Bone Disease

Splints These are the most common forms of bone disease. The cause is a small bony growth which forms on the side of the splint or cannon bone. A swelling, which is usually inflamed, will appear over the lump while it is still forming. Once it has settled down, however, it will seldom cause any trouble. This minor disorder is most common in young horses new to exercise.

Sore Shins These are also common in young horses new to work and are likely to result in lameness. They are caused by repeated work allowing too much pressure on the juvenile cannon bones, causing pain, swelling and inflammation.

Degenerative Joint Disease or Arthritis As in human beings, this is caused by wear and tear, and is often a result of old age. It can occur in any of the limb joints in the form of *ringbone*, which is a bony enlargement of the pastern bones or coronet, and *sidebone*, a calcification of the lateral cartilage near to the heel. This is a chronic condition aggravated if the horse brushes against it. Another condition affecting the hock is *bone spavin*; this causes lameness which in the early stages wears

off during exercise. As the disease progresses, however, the bones completely fuse together causing chronic lameness. In all these conditions analgesic anti-inflammatory drugs may be prescribed to ease the pain.

Bursal Enlargements These are soft swellings which are usually caused by wear, tear or strain, and occasionally by poor conformation: they do not always cause lameness but should be treated as a warning sign that the horse is being either overworked or neglected.

Windgalls are swellings that occur above and to the sides of the fetlock joint. They are usually at their worst during rest, but do not usually cause lameness. A *thoroughpin* is a distension of the tendon sheath, which protrudes

either side of the hock and can be caused by poor conformation and are a warning of a strain. They should be treated with cold hosing followed by massage; an embrocation may be prescribed by your vet. *Bog spavin* is a swelling which forms on the inside of the hock and causes no pain. Some swellings can be caused by insufficient bedding: when the horse lies down, his joints may rest on hard ground causing *capped hock* and *capped elbow*. These swellings can be quite large, but are usually painless; however, they are a disfigurement caused by neglect. Make sure your horse has a deep and comfortable bed to lie on.

Lymphangitis Caused by an infection entering a wound, this can also develop through insufficient exercise or overfeeding. Symptoms present in the form of a large swelling of one or both hindlegs due to inflammation of the walls of the lymphatic vessels. The horse will be in obvious pain and reluctant to walk or put weight on his legs; he may have a slight temperature. This should be treated by your vet who will prescribe antibiotics and anti-inflammatory drugs.

Disorders of the Foot
The horse's foot is an extremely complex shock absorber which must deal with the combined weight of both horse and rider. It has to be tough enough to cope with hard ground and rough terrain. But it isn't a perfect structure and is prone to disease and disorders which cause around 90 per cent of lameness: this should be the first thing you think of in the event of a horse becoming lame.

Maintaining a horse's feet in a healthy condition, with twice-daily checks and regular shoeing, will dramatically reduce the incidence of problems occurring; once a week, a good disinfectant scrub is recommended.

Corns These are bruises to the area below the heel of the foot and are usually caused by shoes left on for too long when they have become too tight. The horse gets increasingly lame which will be more obvious on hard or uneven ground. The surrounding area of horn may be discoloured, indicating the presence of blood. Your farrier will be able to cure this problem with regular corrective shoeing.

Laminitis Particularly common in ponies, though it occasionally occurs in horses as well. It is caused by too much grass combined with lack of exercise, which causes a release of toxins into the system, which in turn cause inflammation of the sensitive tissues (*laminae*) within the foot. Because these are contained within the hoof, the pain in excruciating. In the early stages, the pony may present

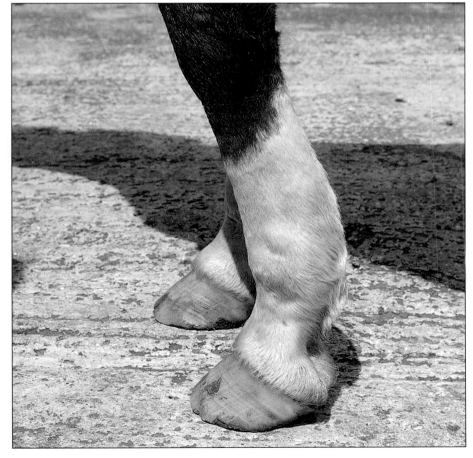

OPPOSITE: Neglect can lead to many disorders and diseases, not only of the feet but also of the legs.

LEFT: This horse has badly damaged tendons and has had to be retired as a result.

slight soreness, loss of appetite and have a dejected look. Later, as the pain becomes more severe, he will stand with his front feet pushed forward, the weight on his heels, or he may lie down and refuse to get up. He may also sweat and blow and have a high temperature or pulse rate. Call the vet immediately. He will administer anti-inflammatory painkillers which will reduce the swelling. Laminitis is a recurring disease, but it can be stablized. The pony will need to lose weight, be kept off rich grass, be given low protein foods and plenty of exercise. Corrective shoeing to keep the toes short will also help.

Navicular Syndrome This can be hereditary, but is usually caused by wear and tear, incorrect shoeing, and is aggravated by poor circulation. The condition is caused by damage to the navicular bone, deep flexor tendon and the tissues surrounding the heel, and occurs in the front feet. The horse will become sporadically lame, develop an uneven gait and will stumble easily. The condition can be easily diagnosed by x-ray. For years, navicular syndrome was regarded as incurable, resulting in the horse having to be retired or

Proper care and sensible husbandry will reduce the risk of many disorders occurring. This horse shows all the indications of good health. (In this instance the horse is unrestrained – not really a good idea!)

destroyed. However, with recent veterinary breakthroughs using drugs to increase circulation, surgery, and corrective shoeing, some horses can be restored to soundness.

Pedal Ostitis This is similar to navicular syndrome, but the damage is to the pedal or sesamoid bones of the foot.

Punctured or Bruised Sole Such injuries can largely be avoided by keeping horses away from areas where sharp stones are likely to occur; however, this is not always possible. *Bruising* is the most common injury and can be seen as a discoloration of the sole of the foot. Keep the horse stabled until the bruising has subsided; don't turn him out until he is completely sound as the injury will become aggravated and take longer to heal. A *punctured sole*, on the other hand, is more of a problem: a small hole on the sole of the foot cannot easily be identified and may heal over, trapping infection underneath. The horse may become lame a few days later when the trapped infection generates pus which, unable to burst out, will cause acute pain. Call the vet, who will locate the point of injury and pare a hole in the sole to drain out the pus, which will bring immediate relief. He will probably prescribe antibiotics and poultice the foot. The poultice should be changed daily until all traces of pus have disappeared. The horse must be given box rest during this time and until the hole in the sole has fully healed.

Sandcrack This is a vertical crack

which spreads from coronet to toe. It is usually caused by an injury to the coronary band which produces new growth. Because of the injury, regrowth is impaired resulting in the crack which, if deep, may become infected, causing pain and lameness. This condition is difficult to cure though there are remedies which your vet may suggest. Careful, regular shoeing will help matters considerably.

Seedy Toe Another disease resulting from irregular shoeing. It is caused by weak horn and a toe which has been allowed to grow too long, which pulls apart exposing the white line and allowing infection to build up. As a result, the foot will become very painful and the horse may flinch if the area is tapped. There may also be physical evidence in the form of black semi-solid pus which will ooze from the infected area. All the infected horn must be cut away to prevent the infection from spreading and allow healthy regrowth. Regular shoeing, picking the feet out regularly and a weekly disinfectant scrub are good preventive measures.

Thrush A common disease, particularly in horses living out in damp or muddy conditions or which are kept for long periods in dirty stables. It is basically 'foot rot', which usually starts in the cleft of the frog which becomes black and moist and emits a foul smell. Only if left to become severe will the horse become lame. Ask your farrier or vet to remove the infected horn. The area should thereafter be kept

clean with a daily scrub and should then be treated with an antibacterial spray or a weak solution of hydrogen peroxide, which should be thoroughly rinsed off. Further infections can be prevented by picking out and thoroughly scrubbing the foot, using a daily disinfectant, and keeping the horse on clean, dry bedding.

BELOW: The feet should be kept clean and should be regularly scrubbed and then inspected for signs of damage or disease.

OPPOSITE: Dusty or mouldy forage can cause many respiratory disorders, so always feed the best quality feed stuffs you can find. If you horse has a dust allergy, hay should be soaked.

Chronic Obstructive Pulmonary Disease (COPD)

The cause of this is an allergy to fungal spores which sets off the condition. The horse will have trouble breathing, will be coughing, usually with a nasal discharge, and will constantly be trying to clear his lungs. Call the vet, who may administer a drug to keep the airways clear. Further attacks can be prevented by keeping the horse on alternative bedding such as dust-extracted wood shavings, and by feeding soaked hay or haylage. Turn the horse out as often as possible.

Equine Influenza This is a particularly unpleasant viral infection which can be easily prevented by a simple yearly vaccination. The horse develops a high temperature, runny nose and eyes, and a cough. Once infected, there is little effective treatment apart from drugs to keep the airways open. It can be fatal to very young, old or weak horses, or, if they recover, they may be left with chronic heart and lung problems making them unfit for work.

Roaring and Whistling A throat condition causes by paralysis of the nerves which affects the vocal cords on the left side of the larynx. This is often a congenital condition. The horse shows no sign of distress until it is strenuously exercised, when a loud roaring sound will be heard as it inhales. Corrective surgery may be an option in severe cases, which involves removing the restriction from the larynx.

RESPIRATORY DISORDERS

Horses are natural athletes, and their respiratory systems need to be in good order. Should your horse appear breathless, or is coughing with or without a nasal discharge, cease exercise immediately as irreparable damage could be caused. Call the vet for an accurate diagnosis.

Strangles A highly contagious bacterial infection with an incubation period of 6 weeks. It effects the jowl region where large abscesses break out under the horse's jaw, which eventually burst releasing a foul-smelling pus; this is accompanied by a high temperature. Sometimes, the abscesses burst inwardly causing the pus to exit through the nostrils. It is vital to get veterinary assistance straight away, when antibiotics will be prescribed. The abscesses can be treated as ordinary wounds once they have burst. The infection must not be allowed to spread to the lymphatic system when it becomes 'bastard strangles', where internal abscesses form in the thorax and abdomen and can be fatal. Due to the disease's contagious nature, the horse must be kept isolated and, if possible, handlers should avoid contact with other horses. Hands should be thoroughly washed after contact.

OPPOSITE: When feeding apples, carrots, or other succulents, make sure that they are sliced lengthways, as small rounded chunks could cause a horse to choke.

RIGHT: Colic is a fairly common condition in horses, so it is vitally important that you follow a feeding routine (see Chapter 10).

OVERLEAF: Horses in hard work can be susceptible to ailments such as azoturia, a serious condition which can cause damage to the muscle fibres and kidneys.

DISORDERS OF THE DIGESTION

Choke Occurs when a piece to food, such as carrot or apple, becomes lodged in the gullet. The horse will seem very distressed, producing copious amounts of saliva which will dribble from his nose and mouth. He will be unable to eat or drink. Look inside the mouth: you may be able to see the obstruction and be able to remove it; alternatively, try massaging the throat which may dislodge the obstruction. If symptoms persist call the vet. This can be avoided by giving food in larger pieces; slicing carrots lengthways and apples into quarters will lead to horses chewing them up rather than swallowing them whole.

Colic Refers to any kind of equine abdominal pain. It is a common condition, but any attack should be treated as serious as it can lead to death. The horse's digestive system is highly sensitive, and an attack can be triggered by many factors. Great care must ge taken with feeding; don't change feed suddenly, introduce it gradually to give the horse's gut time to acclimatize, and introduce it to new grazing gradually. Don't exercise immediately after feeding, keep to a strict worming programme and make sure that the horse has regular dental checks as he may have trouble chewing food properly. If he is a bed-eater, change over to wood shavings, as

63

DENTISTRY

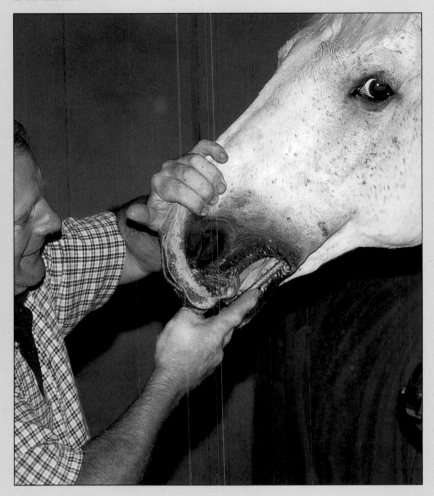

Horses' teeth should be checked at least twice a year by a vet or qualifed horse dentist. Although most horses will accept it, some find teeth-rasping a traumatic experience and it may be difficult to regain their confidence once they have been frightened. This can have further repercussions, making it more difficult to administer wormers or other drugs by mouth. You should ensure that the horse is well-mannered and will allow his head to be handled easily; patience and tact on the practitioner's part is then generally all that is necessary. Tell your vet in advance if the horse is head-shy, or has had a bad experience, as it may well be better to sedate him in the advance rather than risk a battle which will only alarm him further.

ABOVE: Teeth should be examined twice a year or more if there is a known problem. Rasping is carried out to reduce the sharp edges which form on the teeth.

straw can become impacted in the gut, leading to colic.

Learn to recognize the early stages in order that full recovery can be effected. The horse may glance or peck at his flanks and he will refuse to eat. He may sweat and his respiration will increase; he may stamp his feet and paw the ground and his belly with his hindlegs. He may also attempt to roll: this must be avoided as the gut could become twisted, doing irreparable damage. Keep him walking quietly and call the vet who may administer a drench of liquid paraffin to clear the obstruction. Once recovered, offer a sloppy bran mash and put electrolytes into the drinking water as the horse may be dehydrated.

Diarrhoea Looseness of the bowels can be harmless and quite natural, caused by rich grass, stress or excitement. However, it can be caused by more serious problems such as worm infestations, salmonella or a bacterial infection. If symptoms are allowed to persist, the horse will begin to lose vital nutrients leading to a dramatic weight loss and dehydration. Call the vet who may take blood and faeces samples to discover the cause so that he can treat it accordingly.

DISORDERS OF THE CIRCULATION

Azoturia This is caused by too little exercise coupled with too much food. It can occur when a very fit horse is suddenly confined, perhaps due to injury or for a rest day while maintaining him on full working rations. The next day, when required to work, the horse may appear stiff and uncomfortable, a condition which will worsen during exercise, causing reluctance to move and even collapse. On examination, it will be found that the large muscles running along the back and hindquarters have become very hard and swollen; the urine may appear dark-red or port-wine coloured. The horse may also have a high temperature, rapid respiration and pulse, and sweat profusely.

Azoturia, also described as the horse being 'set-fast' or 'tied-up', is caused by the ineffective breakdown of sugar in the muscles which, in turn, causes a build-up of lactic acid, leading to great pain. It is a serious condition: the circulation finds it difficult to remove the lactic acid, which causes damage to the muscle fibres and kidneys. Take the horse off the high-energy diet straight away and keep him warm with plenty of rugs; this will help increase the circulation. Meanwhile, call the vet.

Lymphangitis (See Leg Disorders and Lameness, page 48 et seq.)

PARASITES

Bots These are the larvae of the bot fly which resembles a bee. The fly lays its yellowish sticky eggs predominantly on the legs of horses. As the eggs begin to hatch, irritation is caused which makes the horse want to lick them off; they then enter the stomach, where they develop into

Horses at grass are prone to parasitic infestations. It is vitally important to adhere to a strict worming programme.

tiny grubs which attach themselves to the stomach lining, where they can cause digestive problems and even ulcers. Eventually, they are expelled via the horse's droppings where they hatch into flies and the cycle begins again. To break the cycle, remove eggs every day with a curved knife designed for the purpose; when applying fly repellent, pay as much attention to the legs as you would to the rest of the body.

Lice Infestations occur mainly in winter and announce their presence when large bald patches, caused by the horse rubbing the itchy parts where the lice are biting, appear. Treat the horse and any stable mates with a preparation specially formulated for the condition.

Mange Has symptoms similar to a lice infestation, though it is usually confined to the lower legs. A tiny parasitic mite causes intense itching, with the result that the horse stamps and rubs his legs against anything to hand, causing lesions which form scabs and lead to hair loss. Communicable to human beings. Call the vet who will prescribe treatment.

Ringworm Despite its name, it is a fungal infection which manifests itself on the skin as circular bald patches with raised crusts. It is highly contagious not only to other horses and animals but also to human beings. Keep the horse isolated, including tack and utensils; wash your hands in disinfectant after every contact. Your vet will prescribe treatment; once the ringworm has cleared

up, wash and disinfect everything with which the horse has been in contact. Check carefully for any further outbreaks, as ringworm spores can persist for years on end.

Sweet-Itch This is an allergic reaction to biting midges and is therefore more common in warm weather, particularly near water such as ponds and rivers. Itching affects the top of the tail, mane and crest, causing the horse to rub at it until bald patches appear; this produces sore, raw areas which ooze a sticky fluid. It is thought that shaving the mane and the top of the tail may help; other preventive measures are to regularly apply fly repellents, to use special shampoos, and to keep the horse stabled morning and evening when midges are most in evidence. In severe cases, a summer sheet with a neck cover may also help.

Warbles These are large and hairy and similar to large house flies. They lay eggs which adhere to the horse's coat. The larvae then hatch and burrow into the skin, eventually migrating to the saddle area there they form lumps under the skin with holes in their centres. In about a month, maggots emerge from these and fall to the ground to pupate, when you can treat the lesions as ordinary wounds. Applying a hot poultice (not kaolin) will ripen the maggot, speeding up the process. If, however, an abscess forms or

A summer sheet will help protect a horse from biting insects.

68

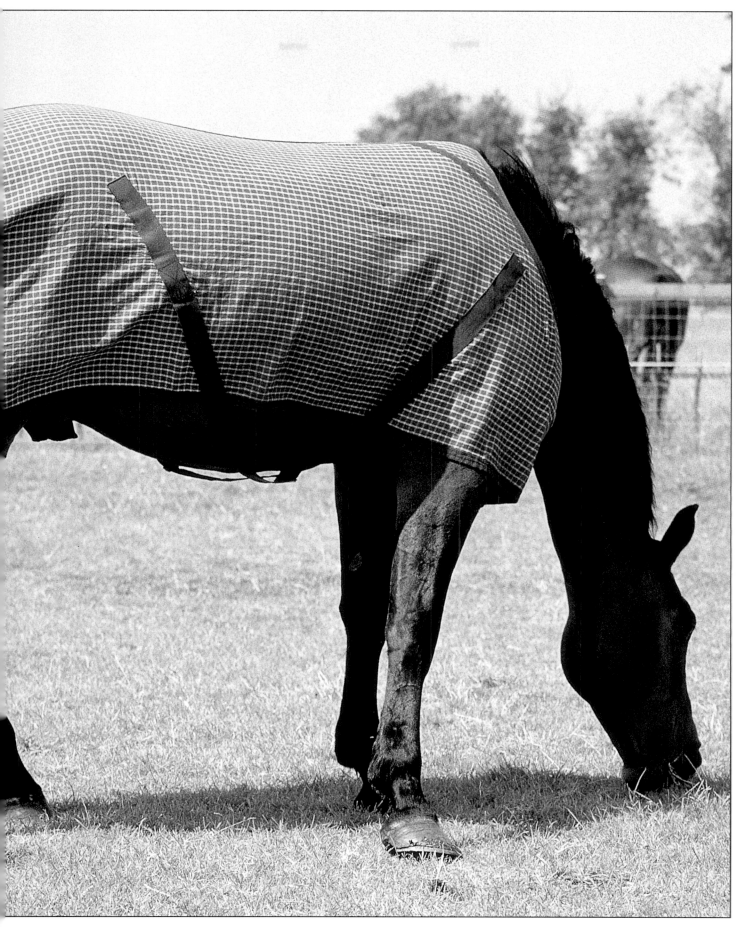

the maggot fails to emerge, consult your vet as surgery may be required. These are a nuisance, preventing saddles from being worn, which means that horses cannot be ridden. Warbles can be controlled by regularly using fly repellents in the summer months. Due to cattle being their main host, agricultural bodies have been making inroads into eradicating the warble fly, with the result that they are becoming increasingly rare.

Worms Regular worming is an important part of safeguarding your horse's health. If left unchecked, worms can cause discomfort, loss of condition, possible permanent internal damage to the vital organs, and even death. It is for this reason that a worming programme must be established. In most countries, retailers responsible for selling worming products are required to complete a training course. If this is the case, you can be confident that you will be correctly advised regarding products and their use.

There are many products available, all dealing with different kinds of infestations. Before using, make sure you read the instructions carefully, and worm all horses living in the same yard together.

Attention to pasture is a preventive measure in several respects: by irradicating harmful weeds, risk of poisoning is reduced. Regularly cutting the grass or 'topping' it is also beneficial; this is because worm larvae crawl to the tops of the stems which are then eaten by horses. Rotating grazing, however, is the best method of eradicating

worms from pasture; this disrupts the life cycle and the larvae die. This is why wild horses do not suffer the same degree of infestation as domestic horses; they roam over large areas, which means that worms are unable to complete their life cycles in any particular animal.

Redworm (Strongyle vulgaris) This is the cause of one of the more harmful infestations. The blood-sucking worms live in the horse's intestine and cause digestive problems, triggering colic attacks. They can also migrate to the blood vessels and organs, impairing circulation to the major organs. The eggs are expelled in droppings which re-infect the pasture.

Lungworm (Dictyocaulus) These are a more common parasite of donkeys but can easily be picked up by horses grazing on the same pasture. The worms spend most of their life cycle in the lungs, where they cause irritation to the bronchial tubes causing coughing. This reaction allows the larvae to travel up the horse's windpipe into the throat where they are then swallowed, eventually passing out in the droppings.

Pinworm (Oxyuris) These live in the large intestine, laying their eggs just inside the horse's anus, which cause intense irritation.

Tapeworm (Anoplocephala) Worms are flat and ribbon-like in shape and can grow very long. They are made up of segments, the last containing the eggs which are expelled from the body. They live between the horse's small

intestine and the caecum where they can cause colic.

Whiteworm (Ascarids) These are most common in very young horses and can grow quite large, causing obstruction in the horse's intestine leading to colic. The adult worm lives in the gut where it lays its eggs which are expelled via the droppings. However, the immature worms live part of their life in the lungs where they cause coughing and a nasal discharge; it is here that they can do considerable damage by interfering with the horse's respiration. Once horses are a year old, they appear to become immune.

SKIN DISORDERS

Inspect skin regularly: a good time to do this is when the horse is being groomed. Skin problems are often difficult to detect, especially during winter then the coat is thick. However, once a problem has been identified, treat it immediately; if you are unsure what to do, seek veterinary advice.

Cracked Heels and Mud Fever
A painful problem, this is most common in winter when the legs and belly are constantly exposed to wet weather and muddy conditions. It can also occur in wet summers or if a horse habitually grazes in boggy conditions.

In winter, the skin becomes waterlogged and chapped, allowing bacteria to enter causing

In the winter months, wetter conditions can give rise to cracked heels and mud fever.

infection, when weeping yellow scabs are formed. In summer these also crack and can bleed. The condition can be treated by washing the infected area with an antibacterial shampoo, which will soften the scabs; gently remove as many as you can, repeating daily until the skin is clear. After washing, dry the area thoroughly and apply an antibacterial cream. Keep the horse stabled until the skin is clear of lesions and has returned to a healthy pink colour. To avoid recurrence, a barrier cream can be applied. Washing and drying the exposed areas when you bring the horse in from the paddock will go a long way to prevent the condition.

If severe, call a vet who may prescribe antibiotics.

Lice (see Parasites, page 66 et seq.)

Mange (see Parasites)

Rain Scald This is a similar condition to mud fever and cracked heels but affects the horse's body. It usually occurs when the horse is turned out in cold, wet weather without a protective rug. The skin becomes sore and chapped, allowing bacteria to enter the skin. Treatment is also similar. In severe cases, however, a vet should be called who will administer antibiotics. This unpleasant condition can be prevented by turning the horse out in a waterproof New Zealand rug.

Ringworm (see Parasites)

Sweet-Itch (see Parasites)

Warbles (see Parasites)

Tetanus This falls into no particular category, but is a disease caused by bacteria which live in the soil and pass to horses via a wound. Total prevention is possible with regular vaccination as advised by your vet. Symptoms include high temperature, general stiffness and discomfort, and the horse standing with nose and front legs thrust forward; membranes will close over the eyes and eventually the jaw will lock, hence the common name, 'lockjaw'.

Stable Vices These are common in Thoroughbreds and others of a highly-strung temperament. They are bad habits, possibly neurotic, which develop when horses are stabled for long periods of time with no outside stimulation, i.e. exercise or turn-out. Once these have been allowed to develop they can never be totally cured, only curbed; they are a serious condition and the horse will be

LEFT: Horses confined for long periods may develop stable vices.

OPPOSITE: Plenty of regular exercise alleviates boredom and the likelihood of stable vices developing.

regarded as unsound as a result.

Vices can be communicated from one horse to another; animals thus affected should be kept out of eye contact of other horses and their stables fitted with adequate curbing devices. They should be turned out as much as possible. Stable vices must always be declared at the time of a sale as detection of these do not form part of the veterinary purchase examination.

Crib-Biting The horse will latch on to the edge of a manger, door or anywhere his teeth can get a purchase, when he arches his neck and swallows air. This will damage stable fittings as well as the horse. Preparations can be obtained which can be smeared over areas of the stable under attack; they taste so foul that the horse is deterred.

Wind-Sucking The horse gulps and swallows air, sometime accompanied by crib-biting. However, he can be fitted with a collar which prevents the action. This and crib-biting are regarded as serious vices and can result in weight loss; this is because the habit takes up more of the horse's time than eating and the continuous swallowing of air may induce colic.

Weaving The horse sways his neck from side to side, moving his weight from one foreleg to the other, putting undue strain on the limbs, which often causes lameness and loss of condition. Placing anti-weaving bars over the stable door will help to prevent the habit.

73

Chapter Six
THE FOOT & SHOEING

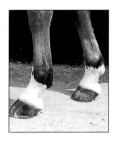

The horse is a grazing animal, not designed to travel great distances at speed, except when fleeing from predators. However, once it was domesticated, it became apparent that its hooves were unsuited to a punishing workload without some form of protection. For centuries, the basic design of the horseshoe has changed very little, with only minor modifications of shape and better use of materials, together with stronger, lighter metals.

New technology has also contributed to the development of shoes to alleviate particular foot problems, such as the egg-bar, which offers support for weak heels or navicular syndrome. The new lightweight shoes can be glued to hooves whose horn is weak, and which cannot hold conventional shoes.

Gone are the days when it was necessary to take your horse to the local forge for hot shoeing. In those days, if it was impossible to get to a forge, the farrier would have had to come to you when, with no heat source at his disposal, he would have had to cold shoe the horse; this is obviously inferior as a cold shoe cannot be shaped as accurately to fit a horse's foot. Most farriers are now fully mobile, with gas-operated forges in the backs of their vehicles. This has two main advantages: firstly, the farrier can come to you; he can hot shoe all the horses in a yard at the same time, which may affect the price to your advantage. Secondly, this has almost totally eradicated cold shoeing.

The job of shoeing has become quite a science: would-be farriers undergo an intense period of training, when they will get to know as much about a horse's feet as any veterinary surgeon. They will also be able to offer corrective shoeing as an important extra. Over time, given careful trimming and shaping, an ill-shaped foot can be corrected to produce a healthier one, less likely to be affected by diseases such as navicular syndrome or pedal ostitis.

Regular shoeing plays an important part in your horse's overall care and goes a long way to prevent disease and general lameness. Shoeing should take place every 4–6 weeks, depending on how much horn has grown; even if the shoes aren't worn, the farrier will need to trim and reshape the feet. Some will offer a refit, where the old shoe is removed, reshaped and fitted to the newly trimmed feet. This is a less expensive option when you are only paying for the farrier's time.

Feet which have been left too long between shoeings can develop a number of conditions:

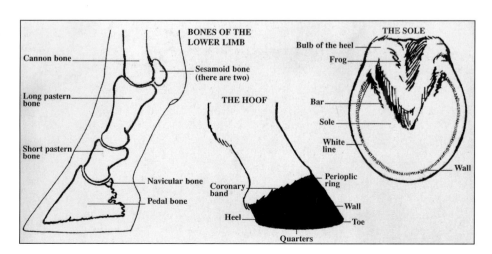

OPPOSITE: Horses which are expected to undertake fast work, such as eventing, must have feet of good conformation and condition.

OVERLEAF: Short periods of galloping on the beach are an excellent method of getting horses fit, as the soft sand helps protect the limbs and feet from strain.

shoes may become tight, causing corns and discomfort; they may fall off completely, damaging the wall of the foot in the process; or they may come askew or twist, causing more injury and pain. Feet which are allowed to grow too long are likely to become unbalanced which can put strain on the ligaments and tendons of the lower leg, as well as affecting the small delicate bones of the foot, leading to chronic lameness.

Make regular checks of your horse's shoes, making sure they are still fitting properly, with no twisting or looseness, and that all the nails are present; check also for uneven wear. Call your farrier out the minute you detect a problem, even if the horse isn't yet due to be shod. Remember that however easy it may look to you, the farrier's job is highly skilled; under no circumstance attempt to shoe or make corrections to them yourself.

Cold Shoeing

This is virtually unheard of nowadays and was mostly used when people couldn't get their horses to a forge. It is not ideal as the shoe cannot properly be shaped to the foot, making any form of corrective shoeing virtually impossible. The invention of the mobile forge and better awareness of the benefits of corrective shoeing has largely eradicated this form of shoeing.

Hot Shoeing

This is by far the best method, as the shoe can be manipulated to closely fit the shape of the horse's foot. As the shoe is heated beforehand, it is more malleable and it is therefore easier to fit it accurately to the horse's foot.

Types of Shoe

Fuller This is the most common, named because the part of the shoe which comes into contact with the ground, which has been provided with a groove, has been 'fullered'. This has the advantage of making the shoe lighter and allowing more grip. Fullers come in two types: the *hunter* which is the most common and the *wide-web* which is commonly used on heavier breeds or those with sensitive feet. These shoes are used on horses whose feet are healthy.

Egg-Bar or **Straight-Bar** Should only be fitted on the advice of a veterinary surgeon as a method of correcting a foot problem, such as navicular syndrome. The bar at the back supports the heel, relieving pressure on the affected area. Being remedial, these should only be worn for light work at a walk.

Extra-Grip A horse's shoes will have adequate grip for everyday work, provided that he is regularly shod. If hacking out usually occurs on hard, hilly

RIGHT: The mobile forge allows the farrier more flexibility as he can travel from yard to yard, hot shoeing as he goes. The invention of the mobile forge has largely eradicated cold shoeing.

OPPOSITE: It is a good idea to ask your farrier to check a new foal's feet; certain deformities can be corrected by trimming if they are dealt with early enough.

roads, however, you may wish to have road nails fitted for extra grip. These are similar to an ordinary shoeing nail but have a small round tungstan tip which is very hard.

When competing, particularly on slippery grass, good grip is essential. Ask your farrier to fit shoes with stud holes. Studs come in a variety of sizes according to the amount of grip required and can easily be screwed into the hole and tightened using a spanner. Only fit studs for soft ground as they stand proud and can cause strain if used on hard ground.

REMOVING A SHOE
Only attempt to remove a shoe in an emergency, i.e. if the shoe is hanging off and likely to cause injury or panic.

Removing a Front Shoe The farrier supports the foot between his knees so that his hands are free. Using a hammer and buffer he will then knock up all the clenches. Next, using a pair of pincers placed between the shoe and the foot wall, he will prise the shoe off from heel to toe, using jerking movements; this is repeated on the other side until the shoe is off. In some cases the

shoe may not come off so easily, in which case a pair of pliers are used to pull out the clenches to release the shoe. This is all done quickly and calmly and the shoe and nails are moved safely out of the way before the foot is returned to the ground.

Removing a Back Shoe Standing with his back to the horse's head, the farrier holds the leg up and over his thigh, pressing his side against the horse's hock which will prevent the horse from kicking out. The hoof is then allowed to rest on the inside of the farrier's knee. He would never attempt to

hold a hindleg between his knees as this is extremely dangerous. The shoe is than removed in the same way as the front.

TOOLS USED FOR SHOEING
Keep a hammer handy to knock back raised clenches and clips when required. This will not harm the hoof and may prevent cuts. A buffer and pincers are also useful for removing a shoe in an emergency. Watch the farrier closely to see how he removes a shoe; he may even teach you how to do this if you ask him nicely! The following make up a farrier's tool kit:

Buffer – Used in conjunction with a hammer for knocking up clenches.

Clenching Tongs – Used to pull over nail-ends to make clenches.

Drawing Knife – For paring and trimming the hoof and frog.

Hoof-cutter – For trimming the hoof wall.

Nail-puller – For removing nails.

Pincers – For removing the shoe.

Pritchel – For carrying a hot shoe.

Rasp – For removing horn and tidying the hoof at the end of shoeing.

LEFT: If you regularly hack out on rough terrain, or do a large amount of road work, you may be seeing your farrier more often. However, the average time between visits for a horse in ordinary work is between 5–6 weeks.

HOT SHOEING

1 The farrier removes all the shoes, which will usually be taken away for recycling. In the case of refits he will remove the nails and clean them up for later. He will then clean up each foot in turn, removing loose matter and filing off uneven horn.

2 Using the hoof-cutter, he trims away the hoof wall to bring the hoof back to its original size. He will probably cut more off the toe that the heel as this grows quickest. It is at this stage that he will concentrate on any rebalancing or re-shaping which needs to be done: this can only be done very gradually over months of shoeing.

3 Using the rasp, the foot is then filed to remove any loose horn and to even up the foot.

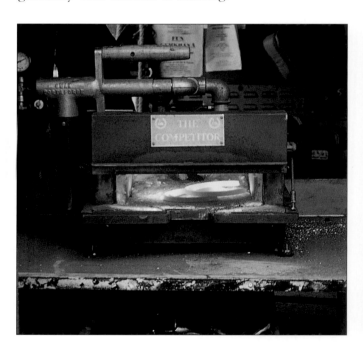

4 The correct size shoe is then selected and placed in the furnace: if the horse is having old shoes refitted, these are also heated. They are left until they glow red-hot. Holding the shoe with the pritchel he then shapes the shoe over the anvil to fit the horse's foot.

5 Once he is happy with the shape of the shoe, he will hold it in position against the hoof. The burn mark which remains will reveal any unevenness which will require further rasping, and confirm that the shoe is correctly shaped to fit the foot.

6 If all is well, the shoe is cooled in water and nailed into place. A shoe has eight nail holes, though not all are usually required. Three on the inside and four on the outside is the most common arrangement.

7 Next, the nail ends are twisted and bent over to form a clench using the clenching tongs. To make it easier for himself, the farrier will usually rest the hoof on a metal tripod.

8 Using the rasp, the hoof is tidied up: all rough edges are filed down and smoothed off. Finally the clips, small tags which are part of the shoe, are hammered into position. These help keep the shoe securely in place.

Chapter Seven
HANDLING

Handling your horse frequently is the best way of relating to him. He has been handled since he was a foal, but he will need to get used to you and your ways. Speak to him often in a quiet but purposeful way and let him smell your hand so that he learns to recognize your scent. Approach him head-on, slightly to the side, and speak to him as you advance so that he is aware of your arrival, then give him a gentle reassuring pat. Never approach from behind or jump out at him: a horse's natural instinct is to flee, which could cause him damage, particularly in a stable. Always be gentle and tactful so that he quickly learns to trust you.

Horses become very good at recognizing their owners and have a way of sensing their approach. Some even recognize the sound of their car arriving and can get very excited, particularly if a mealtime is approaching.

Handling your horse confidently can only be learned by experience; by keeping to the following guidelines you can be sure that a safe and happy relationship will ensue.

BELOW: A horse at home in familar surroundings is usually calm, obedient and can be handled in a headcollar.

OPPOSITE: During competition, the horse may become a little restless or excitable before his event. Therefore, it is imperative that you handle the horse confidently, and for this a bridle will offer extra control.

CATCHING A HORSE IN THE STABLE

Approach from the front, then quietly move to the nearside of the head. Slip the lead rope around the neck to form a loop; this will offer some control if the horse decides to move away. Then hold the headcollar on either side and slip it over the nose; then, using your right hand, flick the strap over the head and secure the buckle. Should the horse move at this stage, don't give up, go with him so that he cannot get away; he will soon learn that it is a fruitless exercise and stand still for you.

CATCHING A HORSE IN THE PADDOCK

Approach the horse slowly from the side with the headcollar hidden behind your back. When you are close enough, speak to him in a soothing voice and extend your hand for him to sniff. Move to the nearside of his head with your back to his quarters. Proceed as for applying a headcollar in the stable. If the horse is difficult to catch, offer a tidbit to coax him. Never raise your voice in anger: this may frighten him, causing him to run away. Don't be tempted to chase him for, after the initial shock, he may come to regard this as a great game.

When catching a horse in a field, always be cautious and alert. It is wise to wear a hard hat and gloves just in case an accident occurs. Most horses are accustomed to being caught daily, so should not present any problems.

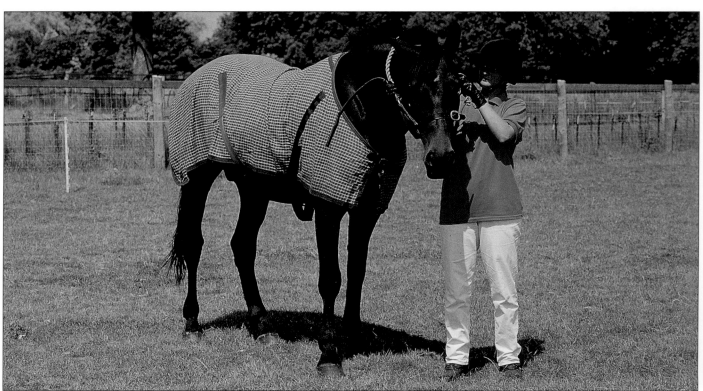

circumstances tie a horse to a door hinge, gate or any other unsuitable object as this is extremely dangerous.

Tie him up using a quick-release knot (see below), which is easy to undo if the horse panics. Don't leave him tied up for long periods: this is not only boring, but he may become stiff and cold. Do any jobs required, then put him back in his stable or turn him out.

OTHER RESTRAINTS

At certain times in your horse's life, other forms of restraint will be the only option, e.g. for clipping, veterinary treatment or worming. When a horse discovers there are unpleasant things in life, his natural reaction is to run away; at times like these a firm

FITTING A HEADCOLLAR

The noseband should be situated half-way between eyes and muzzle. It should be neither too loose nor too tight. A good guide is that you should be able to insert three fingers between the noseband and the nose. Only put a headcollar on a horse to lead him or as a means of restraint. Take it off when he is in the stable or paddock, as it could easily get caught up, causing fright or injury.

TYING-UP

When tying a horse up, it should never be directly to a ring: horses are immensely strong and in the event of them breaking away can panic and do considerable damage. Tie a piece of baling twine to the ring and secure him to that; it will break before doing any damage. Never under any

hand may not be enough.

Start off gently: you could try simple distractions, such as a tasty tidbit, while lifting a front leg up may disable him temporarily, allowing for quick treatment; but a bridle or lunge cavesson will offer more effective control. However, when all else fails you can resort to a metal twitch. Fitted carefully and firmly to the nose, it appears to induce a trance-like state, making a horse oblivious to the unpleasant procedure. There is scientific evidence to suggest that the process triggers the release of endorphins, natural painkillers which are released into the bloodstream and produce a calming effect. Sometimes, however, even this isn't enough: ask your vet to administer a mild sedative.

LEADING A HORSE

In the Yard Your horse should be taught to behave when it is being led; a headcollar is fine in the stableyard. Because most people are right-handed, it is usual to walk on the horse's nearside, which means that your controlling arm is nearest the horse; if you are left-handed you may feel more comfortable the other way round. Place your controlling arm on the lead rope about 12in (30cm) from the headcollar, your left hand holding the end. Never ever wrap the rope around your hand; should the horse flee in panic you could be dragged along and easily break fingers. Always wear gloves when performing this operation as rope burns can be very painful.

Don't pull a horse around sharply: horses aren't supple enough to cope and may be injured. If he stops and refuses to go forward, don't pull on him as if it were a tug o'war; stand beside him and encourage him forward with pushing motions, speaking to him in a gentle voice.

On the Road Before attempting to lead a horse onto a road, make sure he is accustomed to traffic. Choose a safe area beside the road and let him look around. He should be showing interest while remaining calm. Practise leading him during quiet periods of the day when traffic is lighter until you are confident he can cope. Remember that a horse which is traffic-shy is not only a danger to himself but to you and motorists.

Leading a horse on the road is potentially dangerous and should be avoided whenever

BELOW: Fitting a headcollar.

OPPOSITE
ABOVE: A horse can be led safely wearing a headcollar while in the confines of his stable yard.

BELOW: A quick-release knot.

possible; when there is no other option but to do so, more restraint is required. Always lead him in a bridle with the reins over the head and held as you would a lead rope (don't wrap it around your hand). Walk in the same direction as the traffic, keeping your body between the side of the road and the horse. For your own safety always wear gloves and a hard hat. If you lack confidence, ask another person to accompany you; they will be useful for slowing down the traffic should a problem occur.

When leading a horse on the road always wear a hard hat and gloves. It is also important that you can be seen by other road users: either wear bright clothes or a reflective tabard. The horse should always wear a bridle.

Chapter Eight
STABLE MANAGEMENT

Experienced equestrians are only too aware of the importance of a well-designed stable yard: errors of layout, drainage, lighting, as well as badly-sited entrances for pedestrians and vehicles, cause many difficulties, leading to a greater and more time-consuming workload. If you are lucky enough to own land where you can establish a new yard from scratch, take the time to plan it carefully.

STABLING

Stables should preferably be built in rows or around a central courtyard. Make sure there is enough space between rows to allow horses to be easily moved from one location to another. It is also important to provide an area where horses can be tied up safely. Horses should not be tied up too near to one another, as a squabble may lead to one or other of them being kicked or bitten. The stables themselves

BELOW: A good routine, feeding and exercise will keep the stabled horse happy and healthy.

OPPOSITE: It is useful to have a safe place where you can tie up your horse while you are mucking out.

OVERLEAF: These stabled horses are often taken out for a leg stretch and are allowed to graze for a while in-hand.

should be of adequate size and, if the location is exposed, should have their entrances facing away from the prevailing wind. The stables should be airy but free from draughts. Horses are happiest in loose boxes where they have sufficient space to move around. A medium-sized horse requires a stable 12-ft (3.7-m) square; if a horse is particularly large, 14 x 12ft (4.3 x 3.7m) is recommended. Ponies can be accommodated in a 10 x 12-ft (3 x 3.7-m) loose box. In larger yards an isolation stable for sick horses is recommended, well away from the main yard; should an infection break out, the risk of the other horses becoming infected is thereby reduced. Loose boxes should be located in a well drained site and all roofs should be meticulously maintained. Stables prone to flooding are a great inconvenience, as bedding has to be constantly replaced during wet weather and are uncomfortable and unhealthy for their occupants.

Stable Fittings Stables should be fitted with specially made latches, mangers, haynet tying rings and, where necessary, should be fitted with grilles (for horses which are liable to jump out or are prone to biting passers-by) or anti-weaving

These sturdy brick stables were built at the turn of the last century and are most attractive. They offer warmth in winter and coolness in summer.

grilles (see page 73). Hayracks, if required, should be fitted at a safe height, but not so high as to allow dust from hay to fall into a horse's eyes. Salt licks are also useful, being ready and to hand when horses need them. Traditionally, water is supplied to horses in buckets, but if they are often knocked over, an automatic, self-filling system can be installed. Toys are available from various sources and are designed to alleviate the boredom of a horse confined to a stable.

Flooring The traditional stable floor is usually of concrete, but it is becoming increasingly popular to cover the concrete with rubber. This provides a warm, slip-proof base; because of this, bedding can be reduced.

TYPES OF STABLING
Today, the most popular stabling is made of wood, which arrives ready to assemble. There are variations in quality, and it is wise to shop around before selecting the type suitable to your requirements.

Brick-built stables are best: they are strong, airy but warm in winter and do not rot. Indoor stabling in a large barn partitioned with panels and bars is also popular; the horses are kept warm in winter out of the elements and cool in summer when ventilation can be introduced. These are preferable for horses which are being kept in countries that have extreme climates. The drawback is that natural light may be at a premium; moreover, horses may feel uneasy with only bars separating them from their neighbours.

98

BELOW: These indoor stables provide first-class accommodation. They are particularly beneficial in countries where extreme variations in temperature are experienced, i.e. they are warm in winter and cool in summer.

OPPOSITE:
ABOVE: Tack rooms should be free from damp and equipped with plenty of saddle racks and pegs for bridles. As tack is a valuable commodity, it is wise to fit strong doors, sturdy locks and a burglar alarm.

BELOW: This well organized feed room has a blackboard displaying each horse's feeding requirements. The feed bins are vermin-proof and have easy access.

Water Supply In the stable yard, a good, easily accessible water supply is essential; it is also important that a drain is sited at this location as the cleaning of boots, buckets and other equipment, as well as hosing horses down, will produce a lot of excess water which needs to drain away. Ideally, the tap and hosepipe should be in a frost-free location and all pipes leading to the tap should be lagged to prevent them from becoming frozen in winter.

Electricity Supply As with all electrical fittings situated outside, a circuit-breaker, installed within the main fuse box of the electricity supply, will reduce injury in the event of wires becoming wet or damaged. Outdoor sockets and switches designed for the purpose are the only ones which should be used. Do not be tempted to economize by using regular indoor fittings.

Fire Prevention Most stable yards store hay and straw which is a perennial fire risk. Store these in a barn well away from stables so that, in the event of it catching fire, there will be no danger to horses. Make sure there is an adequate amount of extinguishers located around the yard and that you and others are aware of the drill to evacuate people and animals in the event of a fire; plan at least two different exits out of the yard. Smoking in stableyards should be strictly prohibited and 'No Smoking' signs prominently displayed in strategic positions.

Security These days, theft is still on the increase; but there is much

Equipment for Mucking Out
Wheelbarrow
Shovel
Four-pronged fork, with blunted prongs
Skep
Hosepipe
Shavings fork
Rake
Broom

you can do to minimize the risk. Closed circuit TV is expensive but effective but alarms also act as deterrents. Make sure all valuable items are securely under lock and key. It is worthwhile investing in strong reinforced padlocks and chains. Fortunately stealing horses is relatively rare when compared to the theft of property, particularly where horses are freeze-marked (page 121).

Storage Areas where hay, straw and bedding are to be kept should be perfectly dry and free from vermin. They should be located well away from areas where animals are housed.

Muck Heaps These should be positioned well away from stables, as they smell unpleasant and encourage flies. They can also be a nuisance to neighbours and passers-by, so think carefully before you decide where to position them. A pit or bunker is ideal for the purpose: it is best if

it is contained on three sides, which will help keep the area tidy. For a fee, an agricultural contractor will regularly remove the muck, so there must be easy access for large vehicles. Do not be tempted to burn the muck: although this is a cheap method of disposal, the resulting smell and smoke is unpleasant and will annoy your neighbours; in some areas burning may even be against the law. Muck must not be spread onto grazing land used by horses as the process may cause re-infestations by parasites which will ultimately be passed back to horses.

Tack Room A neat, tidy and well planned tack room is essential for storing and cleaning tack. Hot and cold running water must be laid on and power points provided. Veterinary equipment can also be stored here and, if space permits, boots, exercise bandages and rugs. Most important is storage for

saddles and bridles which are often the most valuable pieces of equipment. This makes them particularly attractive to thieves as they have a good secondhand value. You will therefore need as much security as you can afford. All windows and doors should be barred or reinforced and alarms and closed-circuit TV are further possibilities. All tack should be permanently marked: in the event of it being stolen and recovered by the police, it can be promptly returned to its owner.

Insurance Policies Make sure you are well insured for every eventuality. Accidents, theft or storm damage can prove costly. It is a wise precaution to insure your property for public liability.

ABOVE: A selection of tools for mucking out straw and shavings beds.

OPPOSITE: Horses benefit greatly from being turned out in a paddock for a few hours a day.

Pest control Rats and mice are particularly attracted to stable yards and can be controlled by using traps and poisons. Handle poisons carefully and follow all instructions to the letter. Rats, in particular, can cause damage and spread diseases, some of which are fatal to human beings. It is essential that numbers are controlled.

Equipment for Feeding
Feed bins (plastic dustbins are rot- and vermin-proof)
Feed scoop (to measure quantities)
Scales
Rubber feed bowls
Water buckets
Haynets

BEDDING
Straw A straw bed is the most popular, as it is relatively cheap, warm and comfortable. However, straw should not be used to bed down horses with allergies to dust or fungal spores.

Stabled horses must be mucked out thoroughly each morning and droppings should be removed regularly throughout the

BELOW: A wood chip bed is easy to maintain and is beneficial for horses who have dust allergies. It produces less waste so is cheaper overall.

OPPOSITE: Have plenty of clean bowls, scoops and utensils.

OVERLEAF: Take time out to spend with your horse. Fostering a good relationship will benefit you both.

day (skepping out). An old laundry basket makes a suitable skep. It is easier to muck out an empty stable so, if possible, secure the horse outside the stable in a tying-up area. Use a four-pronged fork to sift through the bedding, removing all droppings and wet straw. Start from one side of the stable and work methodically through the

whole. Pile all the straw up in one corner and sweep the floor thoroughly. If convenient, let the floor dry for a while before putting the bed back down. From the pile in the corner, fork the straw into the centre of the stable, laying the bed down and flattening it. Shake up a new, clean bale of straw and spread it over the whole bed, placing the

bulk of it around the edges of the stable in the form of banks. These will help prevent draughts and shield horses from injury when lying down. Make sure you add an adequate amount of clean straw, as a deep, clean bed is more economical in the long run and will be warmer and more comfortable. Some horses develop the habit of eating their beds. This should be discouraged as impacted straw in a horse's stomach may cause colic. To stop this, try mixing the new with the existing straw, which will make it less palatable. Finally, it is a good idea to regularly remove (perhaps once a week) all the straw from the stable and disinfect the floor. Once the floor is dry, the bed can be put back again.

BEDDING

Wood Shavings and Paper Beds
Both varieties come in plastic-wrapped bales which are convenient and clean to handle, so much so that they can be transported in the back of an ordinary car without making a mess. Depending upon how much your horse dirties his bed and how often he is turned out to grass, you will find that approximately one or two bales a week will suffice. Price will vary from place to place, but generally speaking the cost will be slightly more than keeping a horse on straw. It is most important that the horse is very thoroughly mucked out in the morning and that all wet patches and droppings are removed. The bed must then be shaken up to prevent it from becoming impacted. As with the straw bed, regular visits to skep out must be made throughout the

day in order to keep the bed clean and fresh. Both beds are great for horses with dust or fungal spore allergies. Make sure you only buy the best product available; the cheaper brands tend to be more dusty, while wood shavings may contain sharp splinters.

Auboise Bed This is a fairly new and entirely natural product made from the hemp plant. It is particularly absorbent and, like shavings, is suitable for horses with allergies. It is expensive to start off as quite a few bales will be needed to establish a decent-sized bed: however, absorbency is so good that the result is ultimately economical.

Deep Litter Bed This is economical as less bedding is used than in a conventional bed. The bed can be started off using either straw, shavings or paper. At every opportunity, the droppings should be removed and the bed

ABOVE: This horse is fortunate to have a large, airy stable with more than one top door which can be opened up in good weather. Something to look at other than the stable will help alleviate boredom.

topped up with clean bedding. It will not need shaking up, but when using shavings very wet patches must be dug out and removed. This type is less suitable for horses which are kept stabled and not turned out, as the continuous heat from the bed can cause foot infections such as thrush. It is essential that the feet are kept as clean and as dry as possible. Provided that the bed is very carefully maintained, a deep litter bed will stay comfortable and odour-free throughout the winter. However, once spring arrives, the bed must be completely removed and the stable floor given a thorough disinfecting.

A TYPICAL DAILY STABLE ROUTINE

7.00am
1. Check horse over for general health and that no injury has occurred during the night.
2. Put the horse's headcollar on and tie him up.
3. Pick out his feet and change or adjust rugs as necessary.
4. Muck out the stable and lay the bed down for the day.
5. Provide a haynet and the first feed of the day.
6. Remove the headcollar.

9.00am
1. Tie horse up. Remove droppings from the stable.
2. Give a short grooming. Tack the horse up and then exercise him.

10.30am (or on return from exercise)
1. Remove tack from horse.
2. Give a thorough grooming, making sure feet are picked out and shoes are in good condition.
3. Put on day rugs.
4. Give haynet.
5. Remove headcollar.

12.00pm
1. Tie up.
2. Check water.
3. Remove droppings.
4. Give second feed.
5. Clean tack.

2.00pm
1. Turn horse out in paddock, if available.

4.30pm
1. Bring in horse from field.
2. Groom off mud.
3. Pick out feet.
4. Give haynet.
5. Give third feed.
6. Remove headcollar.

8.00pm
1. Tie up.
2. Remove droppings.
3. Check rugs.
4. Top-up water, if necessary.
5. Refill haynet, if necessary.
6. Give fourth feed.
7. Remove headcollar.

NOTE: If you are a busy person and have sole charge of your horse, the above stable routine can be condensed into a morning and evening visit with turn-out during the intervening period.

Chapter Nine
KEEPING HORSES AT GRASS

Horses are at their happiest out in a field. This is no surprise, as a grazing horse is as close as he can get to his natural environment. Horses kept in stables for hours on end, particularly with insufficent exercise, often suffer from boredom and develop stress-related habits such as wind-sucking and weaving (page 73). Ideally, horses should be turned out on a daily basis, where they can exercise freely: this means that they will be fitter than the stable-kept horse, and not overfresh when they come to be ridden.

However, there are disadvantages in keeping a horse

BELOW: This horse is so at home in his paddock that he feels able to stretch right out for a good rest.

OPPOSITE: Good-quality grass is essential for mares with foals. Grass contains all the nutrients a horse needs to grow.

This horse is enjoying a good roll in the grass. There is a look of real contentment on his face.

at grass, which is why the majority of people prefer to keep them partly in a stable and partly out to grass, as it is difficult to regulate the weight of a grass-kept animal. During the spring and summer, when the grass is rich, horses put on weight rapidly, which can interfere with the exercise routine for two reasons. Firstly, it is dangerous for a horse to be ridden with a bellyful of grass; secondly, an overweight one will be more subject to strains. In the winter, grass-kept animals grow thick coats which protect them from the elements. This can make fast exercise difficult, as the thick coat causes the horse to sweat profusely when ridden in excess of walking for any length of time. Clipping in winter is not really advisable as the horse needs to retain all his natural protection. Horses at grass

Rolling

Horses love to roll and turning them out to paddock will allow them to do this on a daily basis. Rolling relieves itching and also helps to remove excess hair from the coat in the moulting season. In winter, a horse which rolls a lot will be permanently covered in mud; however, this acts as extra insulation against the elements.

are often muddy and greasy: while this may seem undesirable to the owner, the horse is likely to be perfectly happy and healthy. Grass-kept animals should not be overgroomed as this removes the natural oils in the coat which are a horse's defence against harsh weather.

In most countries, horses are quite happy to be kept at grass all year round. This is not an excuse for neglecting them. In fact, a grass-kept horse needs to be carefully monitored and checked over at least twice a day.

All horses need extra attention in winter in terms of food and shelter, but native horses and ponies out at grass tend to fare better than other breeds, as they have already become acclimatized. Other breeds such as Thoroughbreds and other lightweights are not really adapted to living out in winter, and will require even more attention in the form of supplementary feeding, extra rugs and a field shelter.

In summer, horses need to be

BELOW: Thoroughbred and lighter breeds are less able to cope with adverse weather conditions. This is because their coats are often thinner and their skins more sensitive than other breeds.

OPPOSITE: Hardier breeds can usually be out at grass all year round and keep fit and well.

OVERLEAF: These beautiful Lusitano horses are running free in Portugal.

protected from hot sun and biting insects. Sprays and potions can be bought or made for the purpose. If the sun is extremely strong, it may be necessary to bring the horse into the stable during the hottest part of the day. Sometimes, a summer drought can destroy much of the grass. If this happens, you may have to provide extra food.

When grass is in abundance, horses tend to put on weight rapidly and disorders such as laminitis can appear, making it necessary to restrict grazing. Electric fencing is suitable for dividing fields into smaller sections. Horses with a tendency to weight gain or laminitis can be restricted to smaller areas than those without these problems.

When out all year, horses require plenty of space, with each provided with at least 1 acre (0.4 hectare).

Horses are herd animals, so are happiest in the company of others. Avoid keeping a horse alone in a field; he may fret or even jump out to look for company.

GRAZING MANAGEMENT

Good management of grazing land brings its own rewards, but it is a year-round task to keep pastures in good condition.

It is best to divide the grazing into sections (electric fencing is ideal for this purpose), ideally three; however, two will do if a limited amount of grazing is available, but the aim is to have one or two paddocks rested.

While one paddock is in use the others can be rested, topped and rolled. Weeds can be killed or dug up and the grass can be fertilized.

Rotating grazing land can control worms; resting land interrupts the worms' life cycles, helping to reduce infestation. All horses must be regularly wormed; it is best to treat all horses in a field at the same time, making sure that new arrivals are wormed before entering the paddock (see page 70).

All droppings should be regularly removed from the paddock, which will help to prevent the grass from becoming sour, break the worm cycle, and generally improve the appearance of the paddock. This is particularly important where a lot of horses are grazing on a small area.

All horse owners should be aware of plants poisonous to horses. Some cause serious illness, while others can be fatal (see page 122). All poisonous plants and weeds which smother the grass should be dug up by the roots and burned to prevent their seeds spreading. Do not neglect this: unwelcome plants spread quickly, so regular checks should be made of the entire paddock, particularly during the spring growing season.

Water Supply Horses at grass need constant access to clean, fresh water. Ideally, a galvanized metal self-filling trough is the best choice. For safety's sake the ballcock apparatus should be protected by a lid. Provide plenty of space around the trough to avoid the possibility of a horse becoming trapped between fence and trough. Site the trough in a well drained location and away from trees so that leaves cannot accumulate in the water. All troughs should be regularly scrubbed clean, then rinsed out. A cheaper option to a purpose-built trough are containers with rounded edges, filled with clean water, which you will need to check, clean and refill daily. Avoid receptacles with protruding metal or sharp corners. Remember that horses need large quantities of water, particularly in hot weather. Do not allow them to drink from streams which run through farmland, as they may be

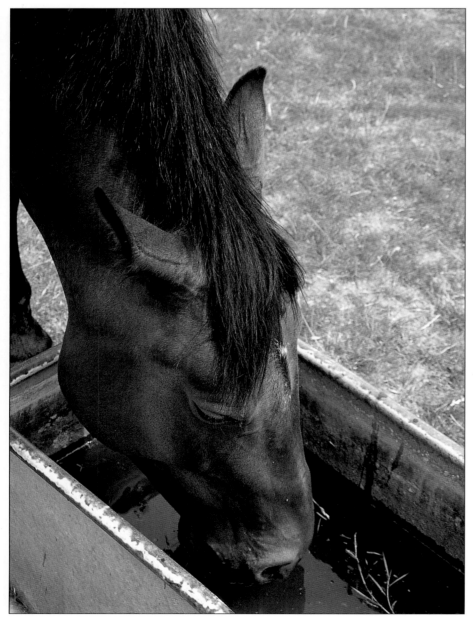

LEFT: Make sure your horse always has access to a plentiful supply of clean, fresh water.

OPPOSITE: This purpose-built field shelter can provide a horse with extra protection from the elements. If your paddock has no natural shelter, a field shelter is a necessity.

contaminated with chemicals; stagnant ponds or any other unsafe source of water should also be fenced off.

Shelter Horses living out require shelter, both from the sun's rays and flies in summer, and from harsh weather in winter. A well designed field shelter should provide sufficient space for the number of horses using it, with a wide enough entrance to enable them all to freely come and go. Make sure the shelter is positioned in such a way as to prevent horses from becoming trapped between a boundary fence and the shelter. It should be sited with the entrance facing away from the prevailing winds. High hedges are also good protection from strong winds, but

it is important that they have been sited correctly.

New Zealand Rug In winter, horses should be kitted out with New Zealand rugs, as only the hardiest will get through winter without one. There are many different kinds and prices vary. Modern fabrics have made them light, waterproof and tough, and providing you purchase a good-quality rug, your horse should stay warm and dry all winter. It is a good idea to have a spare in reserve to allow for repair to damage.

Gates and Fencing This is imperative to keep horses safe and protected from injury.

The best form is wooden post and rail which, with a hedge

behind it, will provide shelter as well. Beware of poisonous trees, e.g. laurel or laburnum, which should be removed or completely fenced off.

Hedges are a safe option and provide shelter all-year-round; however, they do require maintenance and the boundaries should be reinforced with electric fencing in case of weak spots occurring.

Post and wire is an acceptable option. However, it is less strong and can cause injury if allowed to become slack.

Electric fencing in relatively cheap and very versatile as it can be moved around where needed. It is best used in its widest form so that it can be easily seen by horses. If electric wire is to be used, hang strips of plastic from it

LEFT: Horses are happy to stay out in cold weather provided that they are adequately rugged up.

BELOW: Make sure that field gates are firmly padlocked.

at regular intervals. It should not be used as an external boundary fence as horses could easily escape if it were to fall down or the electricity supply fail.

Fences made from sheep wire or barbed wire are dangerous and should be avoided at all costs.

Security

Horse theft is sadly a fact of life: make sure that all external field gates are fitted with tamper-proof chains and padlocks. These are worth the expense for peace of mind. Chains and padlocks should be fitted at the opening and also where the gate or gates are fastened to the hinges to prevent thieves from lifting gates right off. Never leave headcollars by gates or on horses: this is an open invitation to thieves. Place a sign on the gate to the effect that all horses have been security-tagged.

It has become apparent that the most effective form of security is to have horses freeze-marked. This is a painless procedure whereby the skin is branded with a number using a very cold substance. This causes the damaged skin to produce white hairs which outline the shapes of the numbers for ever more. It can be placed out of sight in the saddle area or on the shoulder. The number is registered in a national data base, enabling it to be recognized not only at sales and slaughterhouses, but also at customs and border checks. Moreover, the horse cannot be passed on to anyone else without the permission of the owner and all the relevant paper work.

Another security method is to mark a hoof with your post or zip code: this can be done by a farrier, but is not ideal and will eventually grow out. Identi-chipping is excellent for small pets, but is not as effective for horses as there is the possibility of the chip migrating to a dangerous location in the body.

Young horses are turned out for a few years to mature and grow. Once they are three- to four- years- old they are brought back to the stable to be broken in.

121

A TYPICAL ROUTINE FOR A GRASS-KEPT HORSE

8.00am
1. Remove New Zealand rug, if wearing one (depending on weather).
2. Check horse over for injury and general condition.
3. Pick out feet and sponge eyes, lips, nose and dock.
4. Lightly groom body to remove loose mud.
5. Check water supply and fencing.
6. Dig up poisonous plants.
7. Remove droppings from the field.

10.00am
1. Exercise horse.
2. After exercise, make sure that the horse is cool and dry and brushed off before rugging up.
3. Pick out feet and check shoes for condition.
4. Give supplementary feed, if necessary.
5. Use sun block and fly repellent, if necessary.
6. Turn out into field.

5.00pm
1. Remove New Zealand rug, if wearing one.
2. Check horse over for injury.
3. Pick out feet and sponge eyes, lips, nose and dock.
4. Give supplementary feed, if necessary.
5. Use fly repellent, if necessary.
6. Rug up and turn out into field.

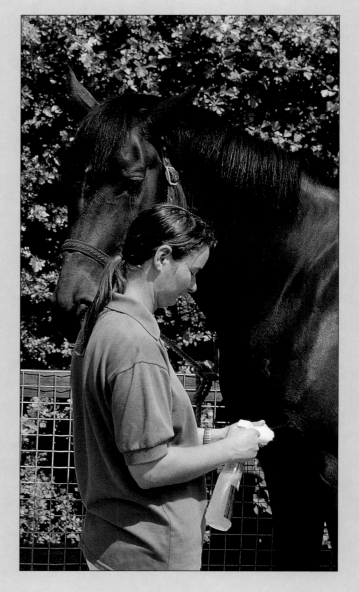

Poisonous Plants

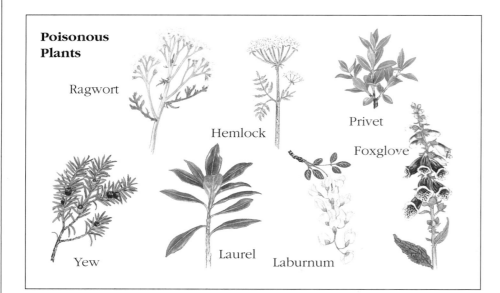

Ragwort

Hemlock

Privet

Foxglove

Yew

Laurel

Laburnum

ABOVE: During the summer months flies can become quite bothersome. You can give your horse relief by applying a suitable fly repellent.

LEFT: Learn to recognize poisonous plants. They should be dug up and burned.

OPPOSITE: This beautiful grey horse is a picture of health standing in his forest glade.

Chapter Ten
FEEDING

Horses are grazing animals. Their natural method of feeding is to browse over a wide area, eating little and often. A wild horse nearly always has food in its stomach, but not so much that it cannot run away to escape from danger. Stable-kept horses, on the other hand, have an artificial lifestyle: consequently, it is our responsibility to make their lives as near natural as possible. The more successful we are in achieving this, the happier and healthier the horse will be.

Instead of grass, stabled animals are fed hay. This should be made available to them day and night so that they can feed or rest as they choose. Concentrated feeds should be given in small amounts at regular intervals

BELOW: A stabled horse needs some succulents fed to him each day to give him the vitamins he requires for perfect health.

OPPOSITE: A horse thoroughly enjoying feeding time.

OVERLEAF: This jumper will require a high-energy diet (see feed chart, page 138).

throughout the day, following a strict timetable.

Every horse has its individual feeding requirements: some need more food than others, depending on size, personality, workload and metabolism. It is essential, therefore, that a close eye is kept on weight and condition, with adjustments for extra nutrition when necessary. In fact, correct feeding is quite a science, and the many different kinds of feeds and supplements on the market, all backed by powerful advertising promising increased performance, rather add to the complications.

If you are considering a horse's diet for the first time, or are worried about that of an existing one, make sure you consult an expert or at least the previous owner. Every horse is different: one may require surprisingly little food, while another may need more than usual for its size, workload and weight.

ROUGHAGE

Hay This is the main source of roughage and is the mainstay of a horse's diet, vital to the digestive process. Hay has a low nutritional content, but due to its digestive system it is possible for horses to extract goodness from it. Make sure that it is of good quality. It is false economy to buy cheap, low-grade, dusty hay as it is less than useless nutritionally and may cause health problems. Dusty hay contains fungal spores which can damage a horse's lungs. Dampening the hay will control the dust, but the fungal spores will still be present and if eaten may damage the liver. Good hay should be greenish-brown, smell

sweet and should shake out freely. If it clumps together, it means that it was baled wet and should not be fed to horses.

Hay should be harvested in the late spring when the grasses are starting to flower. It should then be stored for the remainder of the summer until early winter, after which time it can be used.

Meadow Hay This comes from permanent pasture which is cut yearly for hay. Good quality meadow hay is greatly enjoyed by horses as it usually contains a variety of grasses, e.g. rye, timothy, cocksfoot, meadow fescue and crested dog's tail. Horses also love clovers and other herbs. Make sure there are no poisonous plants present, such as

BELOW: Hay will make up the bulk of the diet of this stabled horse. It should always be of top quality and dust-free.

OPPOSITE: This showjumper is full of vitality and enthusiasm. His owner has planned his diet in accordance with the exercise he receives.

ragwort. If possible, and if there is any doubt regarding quality, inspect the pasture before the hay is cut and baled.

Seed Hay This, as the name implies, is grown from seed as a crop. Seed hay has a higher nutritional value than meadow hay and is very good for horses, provided the quality is good.

129

Soaked Hay This should be fed to horses allergic to dust and spores and is also beneficial for those suffering from coughs or colds. The easiest way of soaking hay is to contain it in a haynet before submerging it in a tub for approximately 12 hours, when the haynet can be hung up to drain. Make sure it is properly drained before tying it up in the horse's stable; this will avoid making the bedding wet. Discard uneaten hay which, because damp, will rapidly deteriorate after about 12 hours. Never be tempted to use water which has been used before for another purpose.

Haylage or Vacuum-Packed Grass This is a substitute for hay and is suitable for horses with dust allergies. After the hay has been cut, it is left for a while to wilt before being baled into air-tight polythene wrappings where cold fermentation takes place. Haylage is more nutritious than hay and should therefore be fed it slightly lower quantities: as the protein content is higher than in hay, the amount of concentrated feed may also have to be adjusted. The disadvantage of feeding this is that, once the polythene pack has been opened, all the haylage must be fed immediately as it goes sour very quickly, particularly when the weather is warm. A good idea is to share a bale between several horses, when it can be used up quickly without wastage. Should you discover that the polythene wrapping on an unused bale has been pierced or damaged, the whole bale must be discarded.

Silage This is the least common form of roughage. However, the kind of silage commonly fed to cattle must not be fed to horses, as it can contain harmful bacteria. Silage is made by a process in which grass is preserved by hot fermentation before being enclosed in airtight bags. As with haylage, once bags are open deterioration is rapid, and they must consequently be used up immediately. As the protein content of silage is quite high, it should be introduced into the diet over a period of about three weeks and should be fed in smaller amounts than hay.

Alfalfa This is highly nutritious and therefore suitable for resting or convalescing horses.

Chaff This is chopped hay, oat straw or alfalfa and can be bought mixed with molasses to make it more palatable. Mixed with concentrated feeds it aids digestion as it encourages the horse to eat more slowly and chew more thoroughly. It is essential for horses which bolt their food. Add a few large handfuls to each feed.

BELOW: Hay can be soaked in a simple plastic tub.

OVERLEAF: Three-day-eventers require a diet full of high- energy foods.

RULES OF FEEDING

- Feed small amounts of concentrates at regular intervals.
- For most of the day, allow access to roughage in the form of either grass or hay.
- Make sure that feed is of good quality and has not been allowed to become stale.
- Try to encourage the horse to drink before feeding, but allow access to water at all times.
- Prevent horses from drinking large amounts of water immediately after feeding or fast work.
- Feed by weight, not volume.
- Make changes to feed gradually.
- Do not disturb a horse while feeding.
- Do not exercise a horse for at lease an hour after feeding.
- Feed a succulent food every day.
- Feed according to the amount of exercise done. Never feed in anticipation of intended work.

CONCENTRATES

Hardy breeds and horses not in work can be kept healthy on grass and/or good quality hay. However, the physical demands we make on horses means that extra nutrition must be provided.

Providing the correct amount and balance of concentrated feed can be difficult to gauge; to overfeed can be just as dangerous as to underfeed. A horse that is overfed can either become too fat, when undue pressure is put on limbs and vital organs, or it may become too spirited and difficult to ride: one that is underfed may become thin and susceptible to disease. It is important to take expert advice. These days, however, the situation has become rather easier, with feeds that are ready-mixed and which can be fed according to a horse's type, breed, nature and weight. For example, there are prepared mixes low in calories and suitable for 'good doers' and native breeds. If a little more nutrition is needed, but your horse needs to be prevented from becoming too spirited, there are mixes for this purpose. There are also mixes for showing horses, mares and foals, old horses, riding horses, event horses and finally for racehorses which need high nutrition to provide sufficient energy for hard, fast work. Clear instructions on how to feed these mixes are marked on the packaging. Make sure you select a well known and respected brand as you are trusting the manufacturer to provide the correct balance of nutrients. Usually, these proprietary brands have extra vitamins and minerals added, so you will not need to buy these separately.

Before mixing your own feed, you will require detailed knowledge of all the various feeds available.

Horses in ordinary work do not need large quantities of concentrates. This horse is largely kept at grass and thrives on this with very little in the way of additives.

134

Oats Nutritionally, these are a good food source. They can be fed whole, but to aid digestion they are better bruised, crushed or rolled. Avoid oats that are dusty and stale, as once they have reached this state they will have lost most of their nutritional value. Some horses and most ponies can become excitable if fed oats, and these should be avoided if this is the case. Horses in rest should not be given oats.

Barley Like oats, this can be crushed or rolled but should not be fed whole unless well cooked. Micronized (cooked in a microwave oven) barley is also an option. Boiled barley is easily digested; firstly, it should be soaked in water for three hours, then brought to the boil. It should then be simmered for a further two hours. Once cooked through, the husks will have split and the grains will have become soft. However, care should be taken, as some horses are allergic to barley and may break out in a rash.

Cubes (Nuts) and Coarse Mixes These are formulated from many ingredients, the advantage being that the ingredients have already been pre-mixed with the necessary extra minerals and vitamins. These feeds do not have a long shelf life, so make sure they are used by the date shown on the packaging.

Maize Has the appearance of thick cornflakes and is sweet-smelling. It is high-energy and can be mixed with chaff and other grains. It is useful for fattening and generating warmth. Use sparingly.

Oats

Chaff

Bran

Cubes

Mix

Sugar Beet

Bran A low-energy feed consisting of the husks of wheat grains. Bran is the only form of wheat which can be fed to horses. It has little food value, but is valuable as a mild laxative. Fed dry it has the opposite affect and can be constipating. It can be fed as a mash to ill, tired or old horses as it is soft and easy to eat. It should only be mixed in small quantities with other feeds.

How To Make a Bran Mash
Put about 2–3lb (900–1350g) of bran into a clean bucket. Pour on boiling water and stir. The bran should be wet but not sloppy. Add some salt and possibly a handful of oats to taste. Place a sack over the bucket and let it steep until cool. Add a few carrots cut up lengthways, supplements (if required), and serve.

Linseed This is the seed of the flax plant. Fattening, and with a high oil content, it is good for the coat and can also be added to a mash. Feed 8oz (225g) dry weight 2–3 times a week.
Preparation: Care should be taken when preparing a linseed mash as it is poisonous if not handled correctly. Soak linseed overnight in cold water, then bring it to the boil for at least 10 minutes before simmering until the seeds are soft. If mixed with a larger quantity of water it can be fed as a tea; with less it will be more like a jelly.

Sugar Beet This is a good source of digestible fibre, has a high calcium content, and is energy-producing. It can be bought dried in either pulp form or cubes. Follow the instructions on the packaging carefully and do not overfeed. The pulp needs soaking for 12 hours – the cubes, which are more dense, for 24 hours. Use the soaked mixture the same day; if it is left for any length of time, particularly when the weather is warm, fermentation will begin, making it harmful to horses.

Succulent Foods Horses confined to a stable require some fresh produce every day. Grass is the most natural food source for a horse, so try to imitate nature as much as possible by taking him to graze in hand for 10 minutes per day. Carrots and apples should also be provided. Make sure these are sliced lengthways to avoid the possibility of choking; remember not to feed too many apples as they can cause colic if consumed in large quantities.

Supplements There are various types designed to be added to feed. Some are intended for show horses, which need to be in top condition with shiny coats, others for horses with poor feet, or old horses. In fact, there is a supplement available for almost every eventuality. Remember that carrots, apples, cod liver oil and garlic are natural supplements which provide many vitamins and minerals and are often cheaper than their manufactured equivalents. When using proprietary brands, follow the manufacturer's instructions to the letter as excessive use of vitamins and minerals can be injurious to horses.

What to feed?
All horses are different, so it is important to determine whether your horse is a 'good doer' or a

BELOW: Ponies need regulated diets: overfeeding is as dangerous as underfeeding.

OPPOSITE: Horses are herbivores and have a digestive system geared to a high-fibre diet.

'bad doer'. The former is a horse which eats up all its food, seems to thrive on very little, and has a tendency to put on weight. The latter is the opposite: it will be difficult for him to maintain condition and he will lose weight during bad weather or when worked hard despite all the care and attention he has from his owner. Bad doers need special feeding: it may be necessary to consult a vet who may be able to find a reason for the problem.

FEED CHART

Whatever kind of horse you have, generally speaking it will need to eat 2½ per cent of its body weight daily.

• Use a weigh-tape (or if possible a weighbridge) to determine your horse's weight.

• The chart below is designed to give a rough idea of the amount of food required for different sizes of horses and ponies.

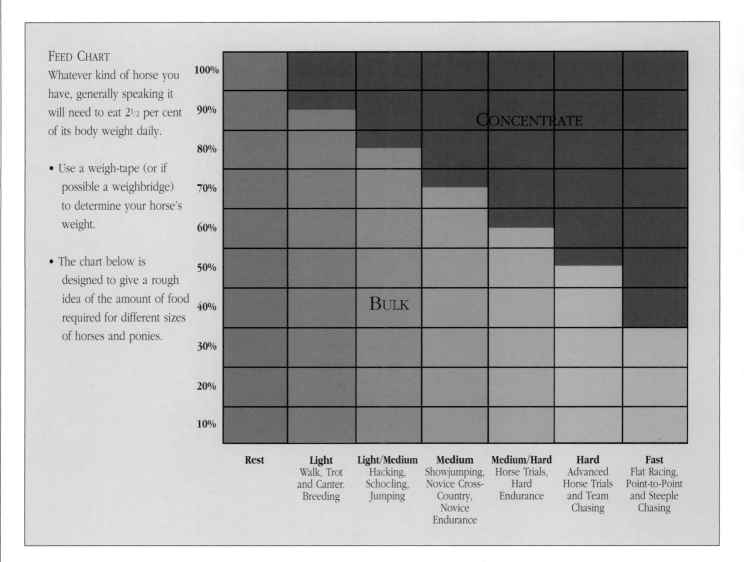

	Rest	**Light** Walk, Trot and Canter. Breeding	**Light/Medium** Hacking, Schooling, Jumping	**Medium** Showjumping, Novice Cross- Country, Novice Endurance	**Medium/Hard** Horse Trials, Hard Endurance	**Hard** Advanced Horse Trials and Team Chasing	**Fast** Flat Racing, Point-to-Point and Steeple Chasing

CONCENTRATE

BULK

TYPE & HEIGHT	APPROX WEIGHT		TOTAL FEED	
	kg	lb	kg	lb
13.2hh pony	255	560	6.5	14
14.2hh cob	400	880	10	22
15.2hh horse	450	990	11.5	25
16.3hh	500	1100	12.5	27½
horse Thoroughbred				
16.3hh	600	1320	15	33
horse Hunter				

1kg = 2.2lb

Consider carefully the type of work your horse will be doing. As a rule, the harder and faster the horse works, the more concentrate he will require. Refer to the Rules of Feeding (page 131) and the chart above for the bulk to concentrate split.

FEEDING EXAMPLE

for a 16.1hh middleweight all-rounder in medium work, stabled in winter.

Weight	500kg (1100lb)
Total feed	12.5kg (27½ lb)
Good Quality meadow or seed hay (65%)	8.2kg (18lb)
Concentrates (35%)	4.3kg (9½lb)
	Oats 2.7kg (6lb)
	Barley 900g (2lb)
	or medium-energy mix 3.6kg (8lb)
	Alfalfa chaff 450g (1lb)
	Sugar beet 225g (½lb)
	Carrots

ABOVE: It is essential that your horse becomes neither too fat nor too thin. This horse is the correct weight for his fitness. As the horse is put into harder, faster work, his feeding régime will need to be adjusted accordingly.

OVERLEAF: A balanced diet is good for a horse's temperament as well as his condition, as illustrated here.

Chapter Eleven
GETTING & KEEPING HORSES FIT

Before beginning any kind of fitness programme, the horse's general state of health needs to be assessed, as any kind of unsoundness or underlying disorder will be accentuated once the horse starts to exercise.

A horse in good condition should be alert and confident with a happy disposition. It should stand evenly on all four legs, though it is normal to occasionally rest a hindleg. The skin should be clean, the coat glossy and it should lie flat. The eyes should be wide and bright with no discharge. A healthy horse will have a good appetite and should be able to chew his food normally. The body should be well filled out but not too fat and should have pleasing proportions.

BELOW: This horse is a picture of health but is in 'soft' condition. In this state he would be lacking in speed and stamina and would also be prone to strains.

OPPOSITE: This three-day-eventer is fit and in 'hard' condition.

OVERLEAF: Unfit horses are prone to injury, so protective boots should be worn.

The limbs should appear clean and there should be no heat or swelling. The horse should be able to urinate and defecate regularly without difficulty. It should be sound in all paces. The breathing rate should be even and when at rest should be 8 to 12 inhalations per minute. The body temperature should be 38ºC (100.5ºF). The pulse should be 36 to 42 heartbeats per minute.

Once confident that your horse is really well and sound, you can then begin to plan an exercise routine to bring him to fitness. At this point it is a good idea to check that injections for tetanus and influenza are up to date, and that the worming programme has been regularly carried out.

A horse in 'soft' (unfit) condition, while healthy, well rounded and pleasing to the eye, is not fit enough to undertake strenuous exercise. It will usually be carrying an excessive amount of fat, not only on the surface of the body, but also around the vital organs, and will lack muscle. In order to bring it to a peak of fitness, it is important that the horse is introduced to an increased workload slowly, as overworking it too soon can cause injury. While steady work is important, it is necessary to allow a horse one rest day per week.

Walking on the roads is an excellent way of building up fitness. However, it is essential that both you and your horse are clearly visible to other road users.

This is beneficial to the horse's mental as well as physical state. If the horse is permanently stabled, on its rest day it should be walked in hand for a short period around the yard to stretch its legs, or be allowed to graze for a while in a safe place. Ideally, try turning the horse out in a field for a couple of hours a day, including the rest day.

A careful feeding plan will need to be worked out. As the horse increases in fitness, the amount of concentrated, high-energy feed should be increased and the amount of roughage decreased (see Chapter 10).

Begin the fitness programme with walking only. Walking on roads is good for horses as it helps harden the muscles and tendons without causing strain. Make sure you are well versed in all road safety procedures. Get some training and take the necessary examinations to prepare yourself for road work. Adequate fluorescent gear is needed at all times on both horse and rider to make them fully visible to motorists.

Walking exercise should last for three weeks. Begin with about 20 minutes and build up gradually to about 1½ hours. Make sure the horse is encouraged to walk

Short periods of galloping will help maintain fitness, but do not allow the horse to become tired or stressed or his condition will suffer.

purposefully, as to allow him to dawdle will hardly contribute to making him fit. During this period, keep a close eye on his appearance. Check that tack is not rubbing and that his limbs are hard and cool; any swelling or heat could indicate injury.

Once the walking only period is complete, you can begin to combine walking with short periods of slow trotting. This can be built up over the following three or so weeks. Trotting uphill is good exercise and helps prevent the horse's front legs from jarring on the hard ground. However, avoid prolonged trotting on hard surfaces, as too much can put excessive wear and tear on the limbs and feet. During this stage, the horse can be schooled

BELOW: During a cross-country competition, the horse will be required to jump and cover the ground at speed. It is therefore essential that the horse is properly fit.

OPPOSITE: Riding the horse in the manège will improve suppleness and balance as well as fitness.

in a field or manège and some short periods of cantering can be introduced.

At six weeks your horse should be fit enough for more strenuous work. If you are fortunate to have access to open country or gallops, more cantering can be introduced. After warming up in walk and trot, start with a 1/4 of a mile (0.5km) in canter and slowly build this up to 1 mile. The strength of the canter can be built up, but do not be tempted to gallop flat out. After fast work, make sure the horse is walked so that it can cool off.

Work in the manège can also be increased. This is quite taxing, so start with 20 minutes and build up to about one hour. Concentrate on suppling movements, including plenty of circles and serpentines. Trotting over poles and gymnastic jumping exercises over grids will improve balance and athleticism and also add variety.

Make sure you don't push your horse too hard. Once he has achieved fitness, have some relaxing hacks and remember to allow him his rest day.

LUNGING

Lunging is an alternative to ridden exercise and most horses enjoy the change. But remember that working in a tight circle puts strain on the horse's limbs, so don't be tempted to overdo it. Avoid prolonged periods of trot or canter and remember to change the horse's direction regularly; time yourself so that he is lunged for equal periods on both sides. The horse should wear a lunge cavesson which is attached to a long lunging rein. He should be encouraged to move in a circle around the person lunging him. Make sure both you and your horse are wearing the correct equipment. The lunge whip is for

BELOW: This horse is wearing a correctly fitted lunge cavesson, snaffle bridle and side-reins.

OPPOSITE: This horse is going freely forward in a soft, natural outline. The handler is positioned correctly.

152

gentle encouragement and must not be used severely.

Side-reins should initially be long and should only exert a very slight influence on the horse's outline. Once he has become accustomed to working in them they can be shortened. However, he should still be able to reach forward into contact with them. Side-reins must never be used to force a horse's head into a position. The head must be positioned in front of the vertical and be unrestricted. Do not lead a horse in side-reins or use them to walk him for long periods, as he could become uncomfortable and develop a restricted walk.

The Rider
Hard Hat
Gloves
Boots
Lunge whip

The Horse
Brushing boots on all four legs
Lunging roller or saddle
Lunge cavesson
Lunge-rein
Side-reins
Bridle with mild bit
 (remove reins and noseband)
Overreach boots

RIGHT: When lunging the handler should always wear a hard hat, gloves and stout footwear.

OPPOSITE
ABOVE: The side-reins should be secured to the girth straps.

BELOW: The stirrup leathers should be rolled around the irons to prevent them from slipping down.

Chapter Twelve
GROOMING & CLIPPING

A ll stabled horses require a daily grooming, which includes care of the coat, mane, tail, skin and feet. Horses at grass also need attention but require a modified grooming session (see page 159).

A well groomed horse will have a much better appearance than an ungroomed one. Not only will it be free from dirt, but the action of grooming the coat will also stimulate the circulation and tone the muscles.

It is best to groom after the horse has been exercised; however, you will need to give him a preliminary groom to tidy him up prior to exercise. This is known as quartering.

BELOW: Grooming will remove dust and dirt from the coat, stimulate the circulation and help tone the muscles.

OPPOSITE: The feet need special attention and should be picked out daily, presenting a good opportunity to check the shoes for wear and tear.

QUARTERING

Work over the horse with a body brush, using a curry comb to remove dirt from the brush. Brush the mane and tail and pick out the feet. Sponge the eyes, nostrils and dock.

When grooming the coat in winter, fold the horse's rug back halfway, exposing only the areas you wish to groom rather than removing the rug completely. In this way you will prevent the horse from getting cold before he is tacked up.

THE FULL GROOM

Before starting to groom, it is best to stand your horse in a well lit area where he can stand quietly.

HOOF PICK

This is a vital piece of equipment. First pick out the feet and while doing this check each shoe for wear, the presence of thrush, or bruising to the sole. Always use the hoof pick in a downward direction to avoid damaging the softer parts of the hoof, thoroughly removing debris from the deep grooves either side of the frog where disease can form. When going for a ride, carry a pocket hoof pick with you; removing a troublesome stone immediately could save weeks of discomfort.

DANDY BRUSH

The dandy brush, which has hard bristles, is for removing mud and sweat marks. Do not use on horses with sensitive skin or on clipped areas, as it is far too harsh. However, it is ideal for grass-kept, hardier animals. Plastic or rubber curry combs can also be used for removing mud, but as

with the dandy brush, care must be taken not to scratch the skin.

BODY BRUSH

The body brush is used next. This has soft, closely-set hairs and must be used in conjunction with the curry comb for removing dirt from the brush. Start with the mane, which can be brushed through in sections to remove all tangles. Once the mane is shiny and

clean, groom the whole body using short, circular movements of the brush. After every few strokes, clean the brush with the curry comb which should be occasionally tapped on the floor to clean. Groom along the lie of the coat: horses do not enjoy being rubbed up the wrong way. Take care when grooming the belly and around the back legs. Some horses are extra sensitive in these areas and may kick out or bite in anger.

Groom both sides of the horse thoroughly and when finished use the body brush on the tail. It is unwise to use a harsher brush, such as a dandy brush, as the tail hairs may be pulled out, thus damaging its appearance.

Finally, using a body brush, groom the head; but first untie the horse's headcollar and temporarily tie the head strap around the neck so that it is possible to groom the whole head. When grooming the head, make sure you shield the horse's eyes with one hand so that dust does not fall into them.

Sponges

Keep two sponges, one for the dock area, the other for the eyes and nose. Use a damp sponge to wipe these areas clean. When cleaning under the dock, make sure you do not stand directly behind the horse or in a position where you are likely to be kicked.

A water brush can be used damp to 'lay' the mane and tail. Brush the hairs gently into the required position; in the case of the tail, a dry tail bandage can be applied and left for a while to allow the hair to set neatly.

The stable rubber is a cotton cloth used to give a final finish to the coat. Polish in the direction of the lie of the coat to bring up a brilliant shine.

Hoof Oil

This can be used for cosmetic purposes to make the hooves shine. It is debatable whether it has any affect on the hoof for good or bad, but used occasionally should do no harm.

158

BELOW: Keep your grooming kit in a handy tray which is easily portable.

*OPPOSITE
ABOVE: Keep a separate sponge for the eyes and nostrils.*

BELOW: Use a mane comb to gently remove tangles and dirt from the mane.

There are other products said to aid hoof growth and strength. However, these should not be relied upon; a good diet and regular shoeing is the only way to achieve healthy hooves.

MASSAGE

Horses benefit from a massage. Traditionally, this is done with a 'wisp', which is tightly woven hay or straw twisted together. However, it is now more usual to use a leather-covered massage pad to tone the muscles, which should be slapped in a regular rhythm along the lie of the coat. Each area should be slapped about 5 times. Once the horse has become accustomed to massage, he will begin to enjoy it.

GROOMING HORSES AND PONIES AT GRASS

Much of the above grooming procedure will apply to the grass-kept animal. However, avoid the prolonged use of the body brush

on the coat, as vital waterproofing oils will be removed, making it difficult for the horse in wet weather.

BATHING

Washing the Mane Horses' manes can become very dirty and greasy and providing that the weather is really fine, can be washed. There are various shampoos for the purpose and some contain fly repellents. Dampen the mane with lukewarm water and wash it with shampoo, starting at the head end and working downwards. Make sure that shampoo does not get onto the horse's face, or into the ears, eyes and nose. Rinse thoroughly, then dry with a towel, making sure you dry the shoulders as well.

Washing the Tail As with the mane, use lukewarm water and a mild shampoo. Soak the tail and work in the shampoo. Rinse well, then brush out with a clean body brush. Swing the tail around to remove excess water and apply a dry tail bandage to neaten its appearance. This can be removed later.

BELOW: When washing the tail, be careful not to startle the horse and don't stand directly behind him in case he kicks out.

OPPOSITE: Hosing the legs can be used for cleaning them, but it is also a good way of reducing inflammation on an injured leg.

Washing the Body It is not really advisable to wash a horse as you run the risk of removing the natural oils which are a protection against the elements. Soaking the coat right down to the skin will make the horse vulnerable for days on end until the skin has had a chance to replace the protective oils.

If the weather is very hot, however, and you feel a bath is necessary, use a special horse shampoo and a sponge to wash the coat. Rinse thoroughly, then scrape the horse down with a sweat scraper before drying with a towel (all this should preferably take place in bright sunshine). Once dry, groom and apply rugs, if necessary, as extra protection will be needed for a few days.

PULLING THE MANE

Most horses have naturally thick manes, though only thoroughbred types seem to have manageable ones. For this reason, it is necessary to thin and shorten the mane by 'pulling' it. Cutting a mane with scissors or clippers should not be attempted on any account. This will ruin the appearance for many months and will make it look even thicker.

It is best to pull the mane after the horse has been exercised when the pores are open and the

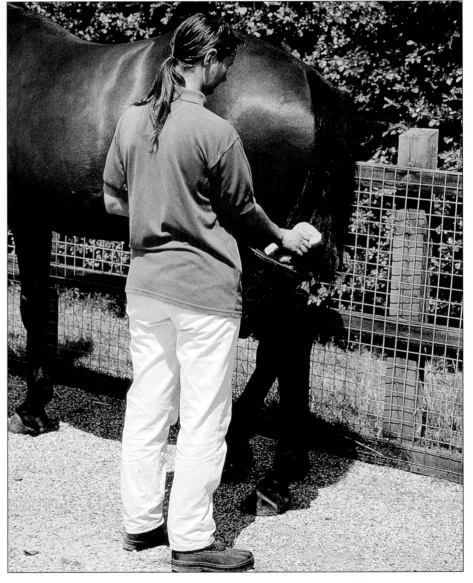

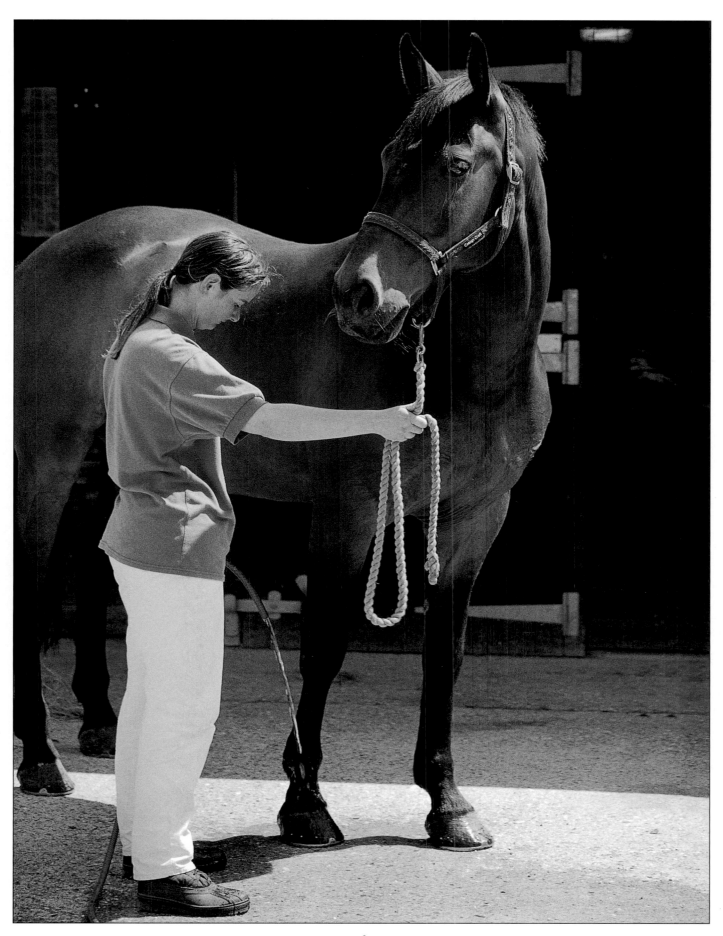

hair will come out more easily. First make sure the mane is well brushed and free from tangles. Starting at the top end, take a few hairs at a time from underneath, wind them around a mane comb and pull sharply downwards. Work down the mane, repeating the process until it all looks even. If the horse is particularly sensitive, pull just a small area each day over a week or two. A well pulled mane will lie flat and be easier to plait.

HOGGING A MANE

Hogging is when the whole mane is removed with clippers. Most horses have a nice enough mane for it to be left natural; however, some have either a very ragged mane or one that is thin and patchy. In such instances, complete removal of the mane is the only way to tidy it up, but it will have to be trimmed with clippers every few weeks. When hogging a mane, make sure the clipper blades are sharp and in good order. Finally, it should be noted that once the mane has been hogged, it may take years for it to grow back to normal.

PULLING A TAIL

Only pull the tail of a stabled horse: by removing hairs from the tail, you will be reducing the horse's natural resistance to wind and rain. Pulling, however, dramatically improves the appearance of the tail. As with

BELOW: This horse's mane is in its natural state.

OPPOSITE:
ABOVE: Pulling the mane.

BELOW: A pulled mane.

For some breeds of horses and ponies, it is traditional to leave manes and tails in their natural state. If you have one of these breeds and it is your intention to show it, you will need to leave the mane and tail strictly alone.

pulling the mane, pull the tail after exercise when the pores are likely to be open. Pull a few hairs at a time from both sides of the tail.

Keep your work even. When finished, and if required, the tail can be 'banged' (cut squarely) 4-in (10-cm) below the hock. Finally, apply a tail bandage which will help maintain the shape. As an alternative to pulling, the tail can be left natural but plaited. (See page 216 et seq. for shows.)

TRIMMING

It is best to leave the grass-kept horse untrimmed as the hair around the fetlocks, ears, jaw etc. provides natural protection from the elements. For the stabled horse, use trimming scissors. Comb against the lie of the coat to trim up areas such as the

BELOW: This beautiful saddlebred has been trimmed for the show ring.

OPPOSITE: For trimming, always use scissors with rounded ends.

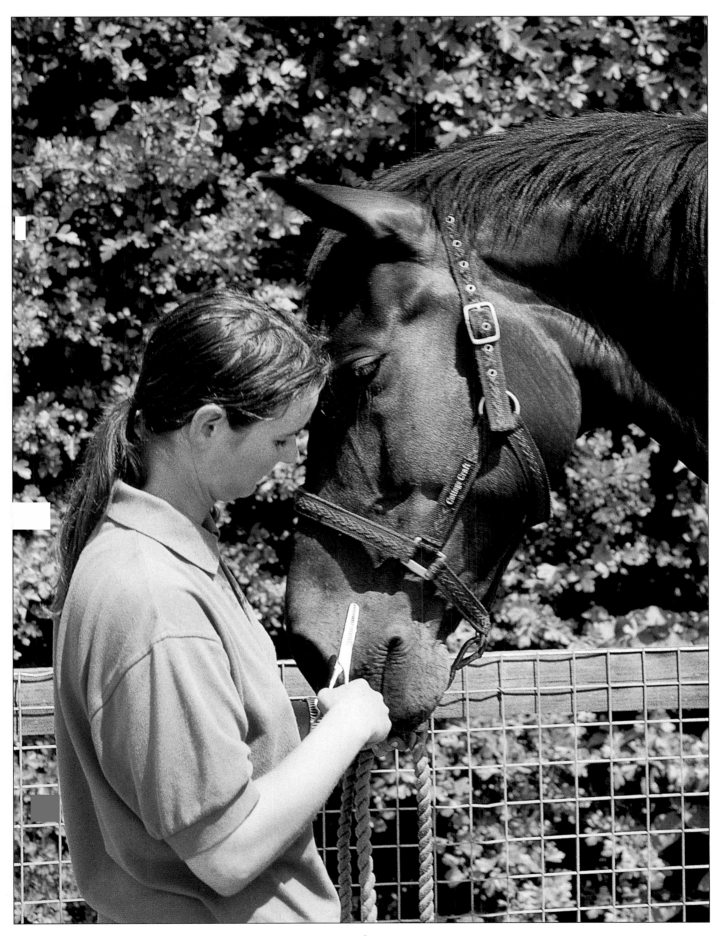

fetlocks and jaw. When trimming the ears, only remove long unsightly hairs, do not remove hair from inside. Also, never remove hair from around the horse's eyes. It is better to leave the whiskers, too, as you will be reducing the horse's natural defence against flies if you cut them off.

CLIPPING

During the winter, all horses grow thick winter coats for protection against the cold. For horses which are not exercised, this is fine, but for those that are worked throughout the winter months, it will be impossible for them to do so without becoming overheated. When an unclipped horse gets hot he sweats profusely, which can be debilitating as well as distressing. As a result he will begin to lose condition if worked regularly in this manner. Another disadvantage is that he will take a long time to cool down after exercise and may remain wet for some time, which is not a good idea when the weather is cold. Clipping alleviates the distress caused by getting too hot: the horse will cool down quickly and will be easier to clean off after being ridden.

Traditionally, the first clip should be carried out in autumn and then when necessary (usually

This horse has a hunter clip. A clipped horse can be exercised during the winter months without overheating. Any sweat and dirt will dry quickly and be easy to clean off.

every 4–6 weeks) until the end of winter. Clipping should not take place thereafter, as once spring arrives the summer coat will have begun to grow and the new coat will be damaged

Depending on the type of horse and its workload, you can choose which type of clip you require.

BELLY AND GULLET CLIP

Clips which remove a small area of hair are either for horses which are not in hard work or for those out at grass. In this clip, the hair on the belly, between the front legs and underneath the neck, is removed. In light exercise the horse can still lose heat, but still retains the bulk of his natural protection. Horses with this kind of clip may be turned out with adequate shelter or in a New Zealand rug.

TRACE CLIP

In the trace clip, more hair is removed than in the belly and gullet clip, but the horse is still left with a degree of natural protection. It is not a recommended clip for horses wintering out, but they can be turned out during the day with a New Zealand rug and given stable rugs at night. This clip will suffice for horses which are in moderate work, but is not suitable for faster workers, e.g. hunters, eventers etc.

BLANKET CLIP

This is so-named as the clipped area takes the shape of a blanket laid over a horse's back. This is a useful clip as enough hair is

BELOW: Blanket clip.

OPPOSITE
ABOVE: Clipping equipment.

BELOW: Hunter clip.

removed to permit fast work; but the back area is left unclipped, leaving a modicum of protection and making it suitable for horses which feel the cold. This clip is only recommended for stabled horses and they will require adequate rugs.

HUNTER CLIP

All hair is removed except for that of the saddle area and the legs. The saddle area is left intact to

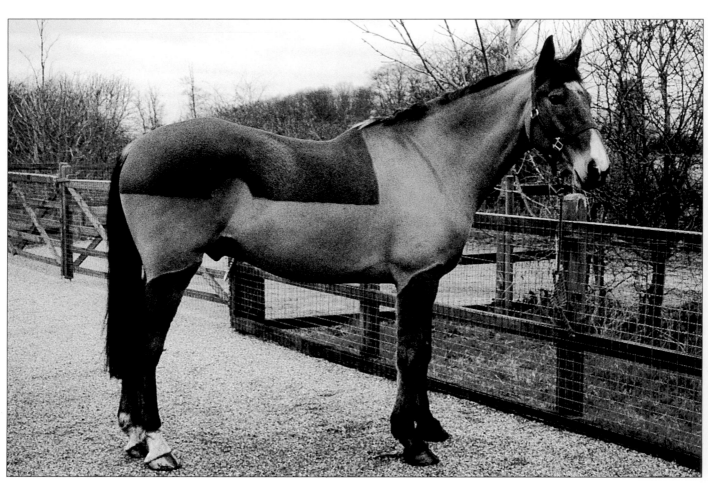

prevent the saddle from rubbing the skin; the hair is left on the legs for protection against wet and muddy conditions which may result in mud fever and cracked heels. This clip is only recommended for stabled horses and they will require adequate rugs. When being exercised, and if the pace is slow, always use an exercise rug to ensure that the horse's loins do not become cold.

FULL CLIP

This is similar to the hunter clip, but hair from the saddle area and the legs is removed. The horse will need to be extremely well rugged up and must be stabled.

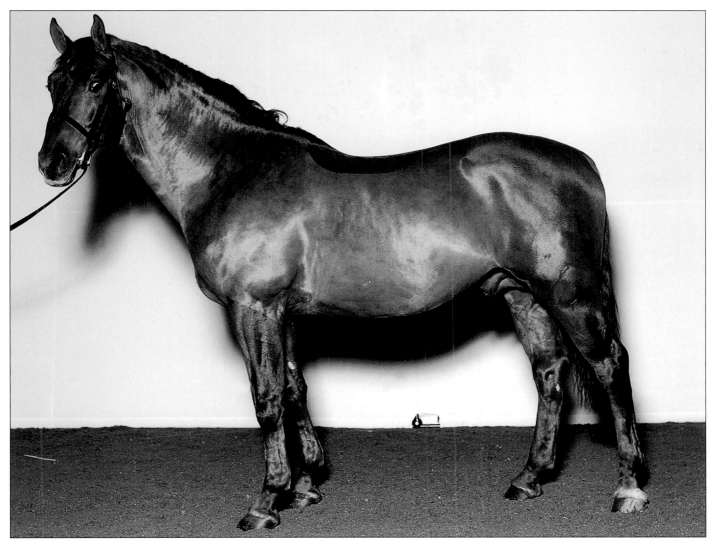

HOW TO CLIP
Preparation

- Select a well lit, draught-free location in which to clip: if the horse is in a location he knows well, he is more likely to be relaxed. Always have an assistant standing by.

- Wear overalls, a hard hat, tie hair back and wear sturdy rubber boots to protect against the possibility of an electric shock.

- Always use well maintained clippers, with sharp blades. Blunt blades pull at the coat, upsetting the horse.

- The horse should be thoroughly groomed.

- Mark the line of the clip with chalk, making sure the line is even on both sides.

- Make sure the loop handle of the clippers is threaded over your wrist; they are sure to break if accidentally dropped. When clipping, make sure the spare flex is kept well out of the way.

- Use a tail bandage to keep the tail out of the way.

- Have rugs to hand. You will find that while you are clipping the front of the horse you can keep the back half-covered, and vice versa.

Most horses are quite happy to be clipped, while young horses being clipped for the first time will usually stand quietly once they have become accustomed to the sensation and noise. When clipping a horse you do not know, make sure you approach him carefully. Ask a handler to hold him in a bridle and try to reassure him. Allow the clippers to run for a while without touching the coat. Once he is used to the noise, turn the clippers off and put them against the horse's shoulder. If he remains calm, turn the clippers on and begin work. However, clipping may be impossible because the horse is so frightened, in which case you may need a vet to sedate him.

Clip against the lie of the coat, the clippers parallel to the coat.

Be extra careful when clipping between the back legs or under the elbows as it is easy to accidentally nick the skin. Take care to avoid being kicked or bitten.

CLIPPING THE HEAD

You can choose between clipping

BELOW: Hold the clippers parallel to the horse's side, clipping against the lie of the coat.

OPPOSITE: This horse is having his second clip of the season. This will be much easier to perform as the existing pattern left by the first clip can be followed.

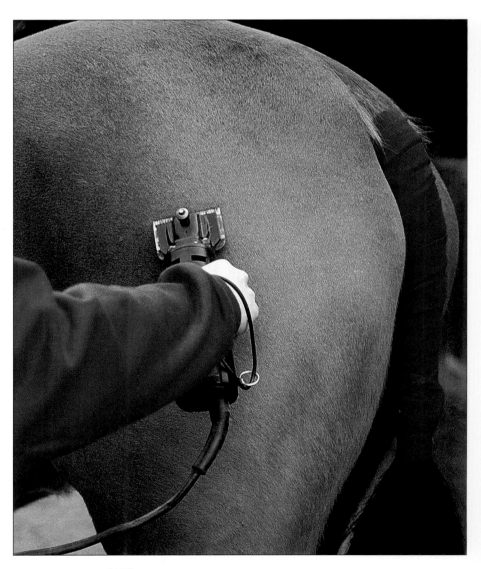

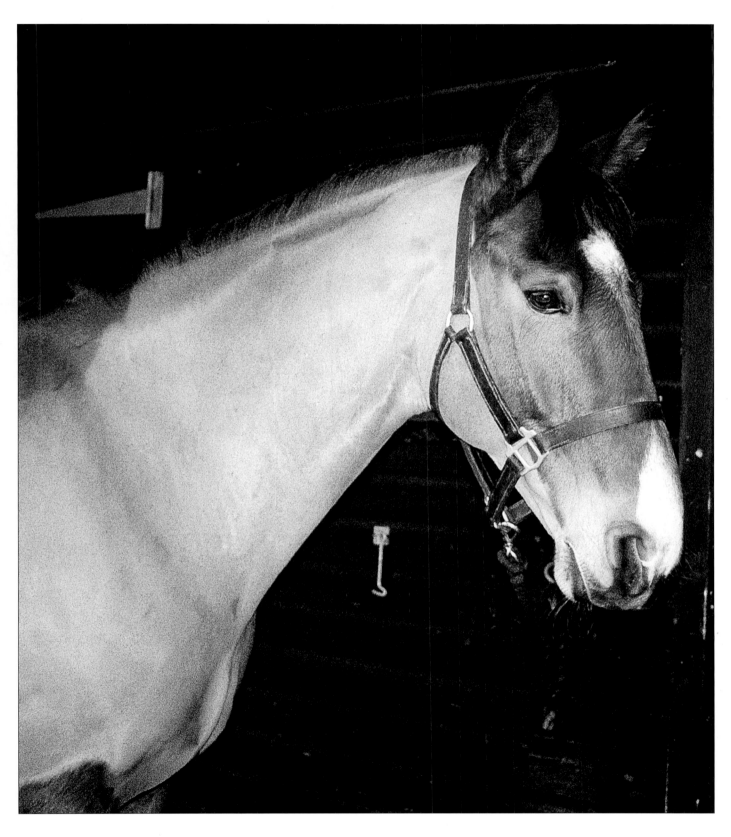

the face completely, clipping half of the face or clipping just under the chin, when it is preferable to use a smaller pair of clippers. When clipping half the face, you can use the horse's bridle as a guide. Clip up to the cheekpieces, making a clean straight line from behind the horse's ears down to the muzzle area. On no account clip inside the horse's ears or interfere with the long hairs around the eyes. Leave the whiskers around the muzzle intact.

Chapter Thirteen
RUGS

Horses in the wild do not need rugs. Their coats grow thick and long in winter to protect them from the cold. However, in the artificial world which we have created for them, horses tend to be more dependent on us. In summer they need protection from heat and flies, in winter they need to be kept warm and dry. There are many kinds of rugs which come in different styles and fabrics. Recent technology has created modern fabrics, which means that rugs can now be warm and waterproof but still 'breathe'.

The best rugs usually have cross-over straps to keep them in place. If the rug is not equipped with these, a roller can be used.

Make sure that it is used in conjunction with a wither pad to protect the spine. The roller should be fitted firmly around the horse's girth, but not so tight as to cause discomfort. Rugs without leg straps must be fitted with a fillet string.

BELOW: This horse is wearing a quilted night rug with cross-over straps.

RIGHT: A summer sheet will help to protect the horse from flies and keep the coat clean in the summer.

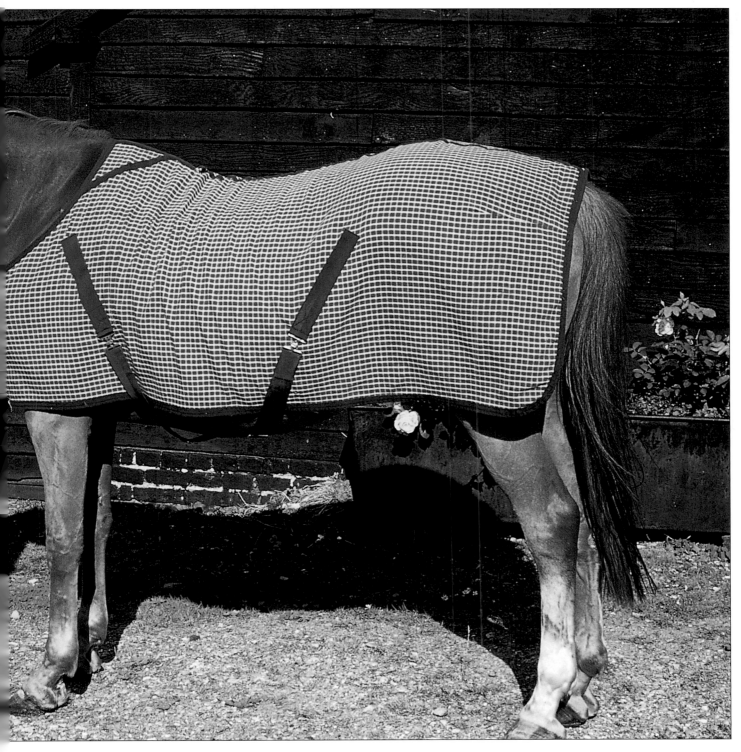

NIGHT RUGS

These should be thick and warm. It is a good idea, however, to have a few rugs of different thicknesses which will allow them to be changed according to weather conditions. Night rugs can also become quickly soiled when the horse lies down at night, so have a change of rugs ready while the dirty set is being washed. Traditionally, the best rugs are made of natural fabrics which are more comfortable for the horse; jute and wool are both warm and durable. However, quilted, synthetic rugs lined with cotton are now popular as they are easy to wash and dry.

When the weather is very cold, an under-rug can be provided, or a blanket may be put under the night rug.

DAY RUGS

In the morning, the night rug should be removed and replaced with a day rug. Traditionally, day rugs are made of wool and should be of good quality. Synthetic materials are now increasingly used, and the technology is so good that even though the fabrics are artificial, they can still 'breathe'. Day rugs can also be used for keeping horses warm on cold days at shows or while travelling.

ANTI-SWEAT RUGS

Made from cotton mesh, this resembles a string vest. Used in conjunction with a light rug on top, the anti-sweat rug is useful for horses which sweat after work, as the air pockets help trap warm air, helping the horse to dry out.

NEW ZEALAND RUGS

These days there are many types of New Zealand rug, traditionally made from tough canvas and lined with a woollen blanket. They can come with or without a surcingle and also with or without leg straps; but those with leg straps tend to stay in place better. Although the traditional rug is durable and warm, it takes a long time to dry when thoroughly wet and can also be heavy when waterlogged.

The synthetic alternatives available today are made from tear-resistant fabrics, extremely waterproof and lightweight. They dry out easily but still 'breathe'.

Turn-out rugs come in many grades of thickness, ranging from little more than a windcheater to thick quilts to be used in the coldest of weather. All can usually be fitted with a neck cover for extra protection against wind and rain.

New Zealand rugs take a lot of wear, so it is advisable to have a spare in the event of the other needing to be dried out or cleaned.

LEG STRAPS

It is important that leg straps are correctly fitted. They must be crossed over and not secured too loosely or tightly.

TOP: Anti-sweat rug.

RIGHT: New Zealand rug.

OPPOSITE
ABOVE: Night rug.

BELOW: Woollen day rug.

175

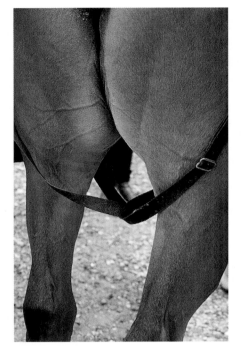

LEFT: When fitting a New Zealand rug, pass the leg straps between the hindlegs and loop them through one another before attaching them to the clips provided.

BELOW: Summer sheet.

OPPOSITE: Exercise sheet.

SUMMER SHEETS

These are used in warm weather to protect horses from flies, and are useful at shows to help prevent the coat from becoming dusty. The rug, traditionally made from cotton, should be secured with cross-over straps and a fillet string.

EXERCISE SHEETS

As the name implies, these are used on horses during exercise. They are traditionally woollen, but can also come in a fluorescent material which is waterproof and affords good visibility during road work. The rug must be fitted under the saddle and secured by the girth. Care must be taken that it lies smoothly under the saddle; any folds in the material could injure the horse's back.

PUTTING ON A RUG

During this procedure, great care must be taken to avoid being bitten or kicked.

- Make sure the horse is securely tied up.

- Pick up the rug and make sure that all straps are tied up and not dangling, so as not to alarm the horse.

- Always put the rug on from the 'nearside' of the horse. Gather the rug over your left arm before gently throwing it, well forward, over the horse's back. Make sure the rug is roughly in position, but still well forward. Do up the front buckles, then gently pull the rug back into its correct position. Then secure the other straps and finally make sure the fillet string is in place.

- When removing a rug, make sure all the buckles and straps are undone before gently removing the rug from the horse's body.

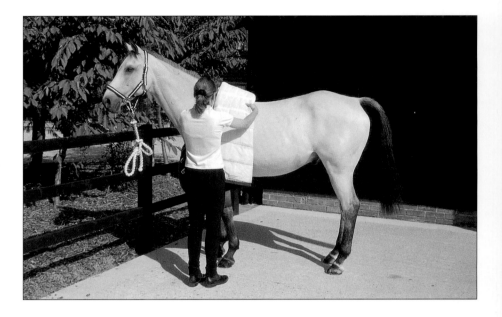

WASHING AND CLEANING RUGS

Stable rugs are best cleaned in a washing machine, but remember to following the manufacturer's washing instructions, as shrinkage can be a problem when rugs are made from natural fibres. Large rugs may be too bulky to wash at home, but can be sent to laundries which specialize in washing such items. If this is not an option, lay the rugs out on a clean area of concrete and scrub them until they are clean, then rinse and hang them out to dry.

Washing New Zealand rugs is a tricky problem as detergent will remove the fabric's waterproofing properties.

Scrub or machine wash with tepid water and detergent. Once dry, the rug will have to be re-proofed using a special spray purchased from a saddler's or camping store. Pay particular attention to the seams.

In the summer months, horses will not usually require rugs. In winter, however, finer breeds and clipped horses will require rugs, their thickness depending on the ambient temperature. Check regularly that the horse does not become too hot or too cold.

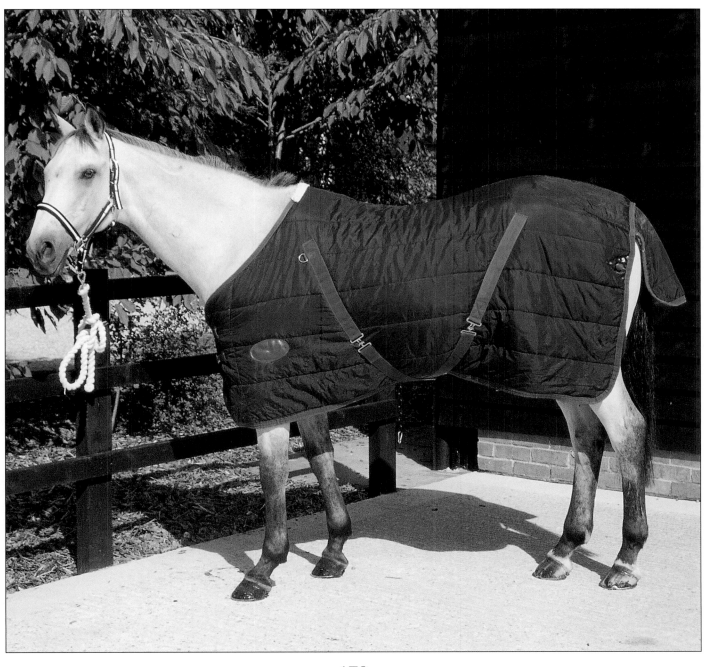

Chapter Fourteen
SADDLERY & PROTECTIVE EQUIPMENT

Saddlery is often referred to as 'tack', which is a generalized term for saddles, bridles, girths, martingales, bits, etc.

It is important to familiarize yourself with the many different types of equipment you will need; it is also important to be able to fit it, as ill-fitting or inappropriate tack can cause injury.

Well made, high quality tack is expensive, so it is important to make an informed choice from the outset. Do not be tempted to buy cheap, shoddy items, as any sudden breakage could be dangerous. It is also important that tack fits both you and your horse.

Make sure all items are checked for quality before making a purchase and be especially careful when buying second-hand. However, it is possible to make great savings by buying second-hand tack; for instance, you may be able to save up to 25 per cent off the new price by buying a saddle or bridle that is only a few months old.

Finally, always seek expert advice before selecting or fitting saddlery.

THE BRIDLE

There are a variety of styles and makes of bridle, and you must select the one that best suits your horse. You may wish to match the colour of the bridle and saddle for extra smartness. Some bridles come with fancy leatherwork and stitching, so if you intend to use it for show purposes, check that the one you choose is correct for the type of showing you intend. It is usual for bridles to come in three sizes for pony, cob and horse, and it is sometimes possible to get extra large. All bridles have some degree of adjustment to enable them to be fitted to the precise size once it has been tried on the horse.

LEFT: This is a beautiful hand-crafted Western-style saddle. This style of riding is still prevalent in the United States and is increasing in popularity in other parts of the world.

OPPOSITE: Points of the bridle.

KEY

1 Headpiece

2 Browband

3 Throatlash

4 Noseband
(with flash attachment)

5 Cheekpieces

6 Reins

7 Bit

REINS

There are many different kinds of reins. They come in different lengths, widths, colours and styles. Select reins which are comfortable for the size of your hands.

Leather Reins These are smart and pleasant to hold. Their drawback, however, is that they can become slippery in wet weather, so wearing gloves is essential to prevent your hands from slipping through the reins.

Rubber Reins In this case, leather reins are partly covered with rubber to provide an excellent grip.

Plaited or Laced Reins These have a good grip but are quite difficult to clean.

Continental Reins Made of webbing, they usually have bars made of leather to prevent the reins from slipping through the fingers.

NOSEBANDS

Cavesson Noseband This is the standard type of noseband found on a bridle and is fitted around the horse's nose above the bit.

Drop Noseband This is fitted below the bit and is used to prevent the horse from resisting the bit by opening its mouth too wide. The noseband must be very carefully fitted so that it does not interfere with the horse's breathing.

Flash Noseband This is a combination of the cavesson and drop nosebands.

BELOW: This American Quarter Horse is wearing Western-style tack.

Grakle Noseband Prevents the horse from crossing its jaw.

BITS

There are a multitude of bits which can be divided into three categories: the snaffle, the pelham and the curb-bit, which is used in the double bridle.

The Snaffle This is the most common, and in general is used in training. Ideally, it should be made from stainless steel which is clean and strong and does not corrode. The mouthpiece, however, can be made of rubber, vulcanite, plastic, as well as metal. Always choose a good quality make and if purchasing a second-hand bit, check that it is not worn or bent.

Try to aim for the mildest and simplest snaffle and make sure it is expertly fitted. Only introduce a new bit when you feel it is really necessary and always seek expert advice. If your horse is not

BELOW: A correctly fitted snaffle bridle.

working to your satisfaction, it is more likely to be the fault of the rider than a problem with the bit. However, if the horse genuinely appears to be suffering mouth discomfort, it may be that the bit you are using is fine but it is the horse's teeth which need attention. In either case, the opinion of a vet should be sought before the bit is used again.

Generally speaking, the thicker the bit, the milder it is. Thin bits can be very severe as they exert a greater amount of pressure over a smaller area. However, make sure the bit is not so thick that the horse finds it difficult to accommodate it in his mouth. The bit should lie comfortably in the mouth and should cause a small amount of wrinkling at the corners, but not excessively so. The width of the bit is important: if it is too narrow, it can pinch the horse and if too wide will be able to move around too much, causing mouth soreness.

THE DOUBLE BRIDLE

This is a form of bitting which should not be used until the horse is working correctly and comfortably in an ordinary snaffle bridle. It should not be used on a horse which has mouth problems. There are two bits: the bridoon bit acts as an ordinary snaffle and is worn in the usual way, the curb-bit is worn slightly lower. Both bits must be fitted well clear of the teeth. The curb-chain should sit comfortably in the chin groove and under no circumstances should it be twisted.

Generally speaking, the double bridle is used in dressage and in some showing classes. The combination of the two encourages flexion and helps to keep the horse's jaw relaxed.

Pelham This is a bridoon and curb-bit combined in one mouthpiece. Some horses prefer the pelham to the double bridle.

BELOW: A selection of bits and a bitless bridle.

OPPOSITE: A correctly fitted double bridle.

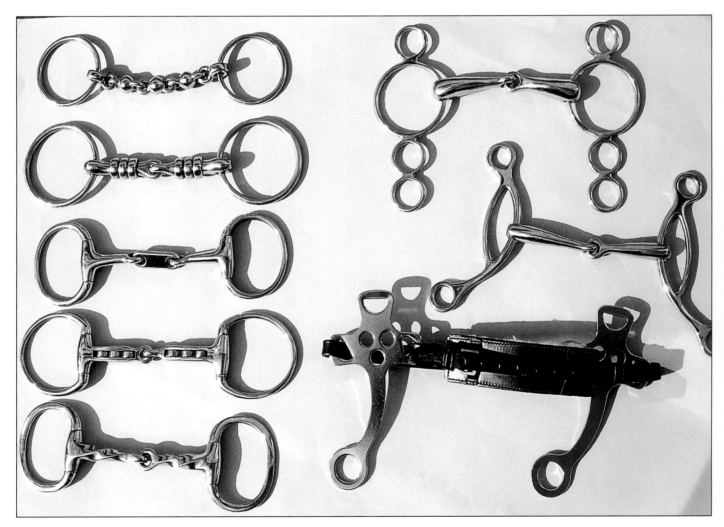

Ideally, it should be used with two sets of reins, but can be used with one if 'roundings' are attached. This is not the best scenario as the effectiveness of the pelham is diminished.

Kimblewick This is a modification of the pelham which can be used with one set of reins. The bit is often suitable for strong ponies and young riders.

Bitless Bridle Also known as a hackamore. Instead of exerting pressure in the mouth, the bitless bridle acts on the poll, nose and chin groove. It is very severe and should only be used by expert riders.

Martingales

Standing Martingale The standing martingale should be fitted to the cavesson noseband (on no account should it be fitted to a drop noseband) and should be used to prevent the horse from throwing its head beyond a controllable level. It must not be used to hold a horse's head down.

RIGHT: The bridle has been fitted with a mild, plastic snaffle bit, which is very kind to the mouth and therefore ideal for young horses.

OPPOSITE: This horse is wearing a pelham bit. It is more severe than an ordinary snaffle.

Running Martingale This should be fitted to prevent the horse from throwing its head beyond a controllable level. Like the standing martingale, it should not be used to hold the head down.

Irish Martingale This is a simple device to prevent the reins from going over the horse's head.

Breastplate A useful piece of saddlery which prevents the saddle from sliding back. This is very useful for horses in fast work when they gallop and jump. When fitting, make sure it is not done up too tightly; when a horse is in full gallop or jumping, it will need plenty of room to stretch forward. The breastplate can be fitted with a running martingale attachment.

CARE OF TACK

All tack should be cleaned and checked for wear after use to satisfy yourself that it remains in sound condition as well as remaining smart and comfortable.

BELOW: First select the correct size bridle for your horse, making minor adjustments to the buckles. There should be four fingers' width between the throatlash and jawbone and two fingers' width between the cavesson noseband and the nose. The noseband should be halfway between the corners of the mouth and the angle of the cheekbone. Check the height of the bit; for a jointed bit you should be able to see one or two wrinkles in the corner of the mouth.

OPPOSITE: This horse is wearing a breastplate with a running martingale attachment.

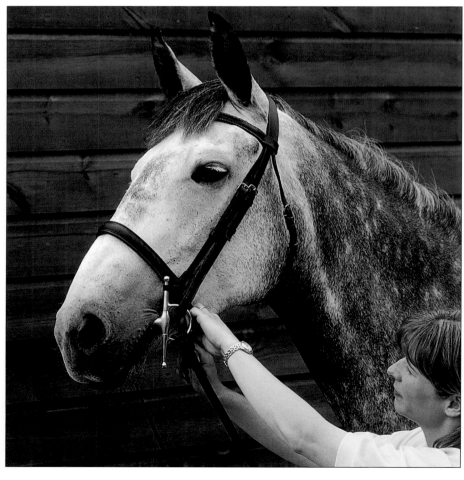

CLEANING THE BRIDLE

When cleaning, check the bridle for cracks in the leather which could indicate deterioration and weakness; also check that the stitching is sound. Any part which needs mending should be dealt with immediately by a reputable saddler or a new one purchased. Take the bridle apart to clean it. Use a damp sponge to remove all the old saddle soap, dirt and grease. The bit should be washed separately in soapy water before being rinsed and dried thoroughly with a clean cloth. Do not put metal polish on any part which comes into contact with the horse's mouth. Once satisfied that the leatherwork is spotlessly clean, the bridle can be polished with saddle soap and a cloth. Finally, put the bridle back together, making sure that it is adjusted to the particular horse's requirements.

CLEANING THE SADDLE

Strip the saddle of stirrup leathers, irons, girth strap and numnah. If you have one, place the saddle on a saddle horse (a worthwhile investment). If you do not, you can work on the saddle while it is held over your lap. With a damp sponge, clean all the dirt, grease and old saddle soap from the saddle. While you work, check it over carefully for wear. Clean the stirrup leathers in the same way. These are particularly susceptible to wear, so check for cracks. Wash, dry, then polish the stirrup leathers. Brush the numnah and girth to remove loose dirt. If very dirty, wash the numnah and girth in soap and water and hang out to dry. Polish the saddle with saddle soap and a cloth, then put everything back together again. Do not apply saddle soap to suede-covered kneerolls as this will stain and cause the suede to go shiny. Cover the saddle with a cover to keep it clean and free from dust while it is being stored for use next time.

LEFT: Clean your tack regularly to keep it supple and free from dirt. Use the opportunity to check for any wear and tear, such as worn stitching and cracked leather.

OPPOSITE: For safety's sake the girth straps must be in excellent condition. If signs of deterioration are found, discard them immediately and replace with new ones.

DIFFERENT TYPES OF SADDLE

It is essential that a saddle is fitted by a qualified specialist; if the saddle does not fit properly, extreme damage can be done to a horse's back.

It is also important that the saddle fits the rider, as a saddle that is too small or too large will upset the rider's position and balance which, as a consequence, will be uncomfortable for the horse. As well as the size of the rider, the saddler will take many other factors into account, such as the horse's age, size and breed.

Once the new saddle has been fitted, remember to have it checked over every six months by the saddler. Horses can rapidly change shape, depending upon age, breed and general condition, and a saddle can quickly fail to fit properly.

GENERAL-PURPOSE SADDLE
This is the most popular type and is designed for those needing just one saddle for flat work, jumping and hacking. While it is adequate for day-to-day use, more specific saddles are required by those interested in particular aspects of equestrianism, e.g. dressage or jumping.

BELOW: This German-made, general-purpose saddle is fitted with knee and thighrolls for comfort. It can be used for all disciplines and if kept clean and well serviced will last for many years.

OPPOSITE: The general-purpose saddle is ideal for riding out in the countryside and will remain comfortable for many hours.

DRESSAGE SADDLE

This has a straighter cut than the general-purpose saddle. The cut of the saddle allows for the rider's leg to hang longer and encourages him to sit taller. Generally, for dressage, the rider uses a longer stirrup than when using a general-purpose or jumping saddle. For those serious about dressage and flat work, a dressage saddle is a worthwhile investment.

BELOW: This straight-cut dressage saddle is being used in conjunction with a square, white numnah, which is traditionally used in dressage competitions.

RIGHT: The dressage saddle encourages the rider to sit deeper and taller in the saddle and allows the legs to hang longer.

JUMPING SADDLE

Riders who showjump regularly will benefit enormously from a jumping saddle. The flaps have a more forward cut than those of a general-purpose saddle. This means that the rider can have a shorter stirrup length which will aid balance when jumping.

BELOW: The jumping saddle is forward-cut to allow the rider to ride in balance with a shorter stirrup length when jumping.

RIGHT: This jumping saddle has padded kneerolls to support the rider's legs when jumping.

SHOWING SADDLE

This is straight-cut to show off the horse's conformation. For novice showing, a general-purpose or dressage saddle will do. However, for higher level it is a necessity.

RACING SADDLE

The racing saddle is designed to be small and lightweight. Even so, the saddle will have to be strong enough to endure the rigors of the race course.

GIRTHS

There are many kinds of girths made from a variety of materials such as webbing, leather, nylon string, and other synthetic materials. Look for a comfortable girth with plenty of strength to it and remember to immediately discard girths which show signs of wear and tear.

BOOTS AND BANDAGES

These are used to either support or protect the legs and there are many different kinds. For horses which have never worn boots or bandages, make sure you introduce them gradually so that you do not cause unnecessary alarm. When removing boots, always check the horse's legs for rubs or sores. Boots should be fitted just tightly enough to prevent them from falling down; the straps should always face to the back. Clean the boots thoroughly after use, as caked dirt or sweat can cause sores.

When putting on boots and bandages, care must be taken as the handler is in a vulnerable position and could easily be kicked. Adopt a crouching position so that it is easier to step back if required. Boots are used to prevent injury, and should only be used for relatively short periods as they can cause rubbing and sores on the legs. Only the best quality should be used as cheaper, badly cut boots can wrinkle, causing pressure points leading to serious injury.

Brushing Boots Used to prevent injury to a horse caused by one of its legs knocking or 'brushing' against another. The padding on the inside of the boot softens the

impact of the blow, thus preventing injury. Horses which move with their legs close together and also those being lunged or ridden in tight circles are all at risk from brushing

TOP: The top two girths are leather, the second two are of a lightweight webbing material and the final is a web dressage girth

ABOVE: Brushing boots.

injuries. Boots can be made from leather or man-made materials and can be lined with softer material to prevent rubbing. Fetlock boots also prevent brushing injuries.

Tendon Boots Usually open-fronted, they protect the tendons of the front legs from a strike from a hind foot. They also act as brushing boots.

Overreach Boots These are bell-shaped, made from rubber or plastic. They should be fitted over the front hooves to prevent injury from a hindleg striking the heel area of a foreleg. They can be fitted with Velcro or straps to fasten them. If not fitted with straps, they can be pulled on over the hoof.

Knee Boots Generally used to protect horses while travelling. However, they are invaluable for horses working on roads or hard ground and those which are prone to stumbling. During a fall, it is likely that a horse will fall onto its knees; these boots cushion such blows. The top strap must be fitted securely, but the bottom strap must be loose enough to allow the horse to move freely and bend his knee with ease.

TOP LEFT: Tendon boots.

TOP RIGHT: Overreach boots.

RIGHT: Knee boots and brushing boots.

FAR RIGHT: Exercise bandages.

199

Hock Boots Used for travelling, they must be fitted in the same way as knee boots.

Medicine Boots These wrap around the lower leg, offering almost total protection to the entire area.

Bandages Great care must be taken when applying bandages; it is important that the pressure is even and not too tight. Badly applied bandages can cause injury.

Tail Bandages These are crêpe bandages which can be applied to the tail to protect it when travelling or to keep it out of the way while the horse is being clipped. They can be applied to improve the appearance of the tail as, once removed, the tail will have acquired a tidy and smooth appearance. On no account put tail bandages on too tightly or leave them on overnight.

After grooming the tail with a body brush, use a water brush to dampen it. Apply a dry tail bandage. Start at the top, unrolling the bandage evenly, then tie the tapes just below the dock. Finally, bend the tail gently into a natural outline, taking care not to cause discomfort..

To remove the tail bandage, undo the tapes and slide the whole bandage off in one go.

Stable Bandages These are an aid to circulation and help warm up tired and cold horses. They are useful for horses which are unwell or on box rest. They must be applied with great skill and not too tightly; always use a suitable padding such as gamgee underneath, and do not use it too

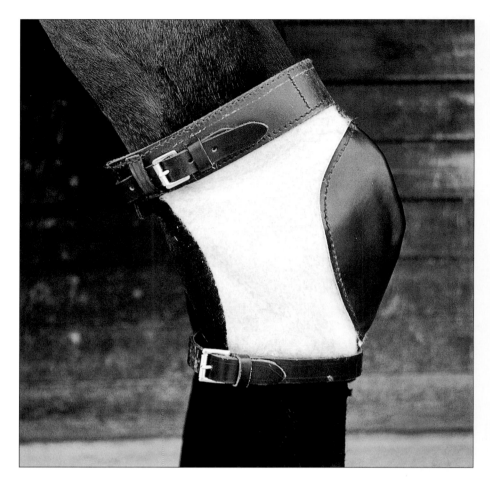

often. Once it has become flattened, discard it and start again with new padding. The gamgee must be cut to fit and wrapped around the leg to lie flat, as any wrinkles could cause uneven pressure on the leg. Begin rolling the bandage just below the knee, or in the case of the hindleg, the hock. Roll the bandage down the leg evenly, applying even pressure as you go. When the coronet is reached, turn the bandage to roll it upwards until you reach the top where the tapes must be tied and tucked in. Tie the tapes at the side of the leg, not at the front or the back, where uneven pressure could cause soreness.

After removing the bandages, give the legs a thorough check over for soreness or excessive marks caused by the bandaging.

ABOVE: Hock boots are used for protection during travelling but should not be worn during exercise.

OPPOSITE: Applying a tail bandage. The tail bandage should always be worn with a tail guard during travelling to protect the delicate dock area. It can also be applied to a damp tail after washing to shape the tail.

Travelling Bandages These are the best form of protection for a horse's legs when travelling in a horsebox. They have the advantage over travelling boots in that they stay put and do not easily come off. Basically the same as stable bandages, travelling bandages must be wound down just over the coronet to protect a horse in the event of it treading on itself or being trod on by another horse. Bandaging can also extend to just below the coronet band.

Exercise Bandages Used to protect the horse's legs during work, they are often used for cross-country. They must be expertly applied as they can cause damage to the legs if wound too tightly or unevenly. Use a crêpe bandage with gamgee for padding. The bandage must be applied evenly from just below the knee or hock to just above the fetlock joint; it must then be wound upwards to just below the knee where the tapes should be tied and tucked in at the side of the leg. The tapes can be covered with electrical tape or sewn to prevent

them from coming undone during fast work. The bandages must only be tight enough to prevent them from falling down. Remember that the horse's

circulation must not be interfered with in any way whatsoever; the tendons must not be subjected to undue pressure.

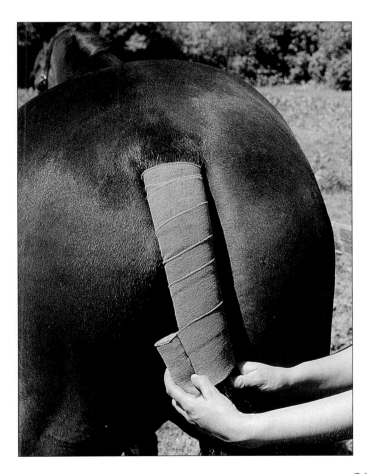

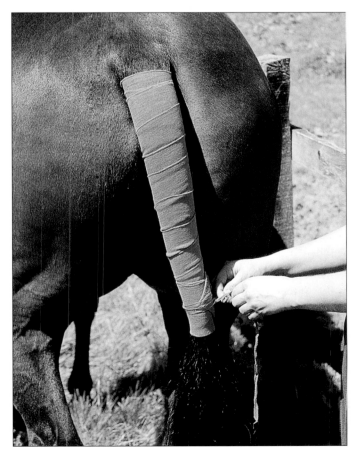

Chapter Fifteen
TRANSPORTATION

At some time in their lives, most horses will need to be transported to another place, whether it is to a new owner, a horse show or a veterinary hospital. For this reason it is a good idea to get them used to the procedure in advance. Horses which travel regularly by trailer or horsebox soon become accustomed to the motion of a vehicle and, provided that the driver is sympathetic, they should never be alarmed or frightened; many owners claim their horses even enjoy travelling.

It is important to practise loading and unloading before actually going anywhere; even during practice sessions the horse should be correctly attired in full travelling gear as follows:

POLL GUARD

HEADCOLLAR

BRIDLE

LEAD-REIN

ANTI-SWEAT RUG WITH A DAY RUG ON
  TOP, IF NECESSARY

ROLLER AND PAD

KNEE BOOTS

HOCK BOOTS

TRAVELLING BANDAGES OR TRAVELLING
  BOOTS

TAIL BANDAGE

TAIL GUARD

It is important to provide the horse with maximum protection while travelling, and it should never go into a vehicle unless it is wearing the recommended gear. It is also important that all rugs, boots and bandages are well secured; a rug without a roller or a loosely-tied bandage could easily fall off causing the horse to panic. In cold weather, the horse will need to be rugged up, but be careful not to cause overheating as this will lead to anxiety. To avoid this, use an anti-sweat rug with a day rug, made from natural fibres, on top. The small holes in the anti-sweat rug will allow the air to circulate beneath the top rug, preventing the horse from becoming too damp.

Short Journeys If you are only going a short distance, horses can be loaded partially tacked up with the saddle and bridle. However, the reins and any other straps must be secured so that they do not fall on the floor or get caught up. Do not transport tacked-up horses over long distances.

Long Journeys Horses should be rested every four hours and offered water: weather permitting, the ramp should also be lowered to allow air to circulate.

This horse is correctly attired for travelling in a horsebox or trailer.

To accustom a horse to the inside of a trailer or box, allow him inside and provide him with a feed so that he equates the event with something pleasurable. A haynet suspended at a safe height will also provide a diversion allowing relaxation. Put some bedding inside the box to make it more appealing.

- Always have a helper with you if at all possible.
- Always wear a riding hat, gloves and sturdy boots when leading.
- Try to keep the horse straight and aim him at the centre of the ramp. Reassure him and give him gentle encouragement.
- Make sure the breeching straps or partitions are in place before tying the horse up. This can be done by a helper.
- Make sure to secure the horse with a quick-release knot and that the partitions are correctly placed to prevent him from turning around in the box or trailer. However, the horse must be given adequate room so that he can adjust his legs to balance himself.
- Be wary of all ramps and doors. They are usually very heavy and standing beneath them should be avoided.

The handler is leading her horse quietly and positively into a trailer. The more regularly horses are transported, the quieter they will become. However, it is important that they are not frightened in any way, as a bad experience can make a horse forever wary.

- Make sure all equipment is stowed well away before the journey begins and that all haynets are very well secured. When leading a horse into the confined interior of a vehicle, aim for the centre of the ramp. Walk with the horse alongside. Do not attempt to drag him up the ramp. If he hangs back, give him a little time and remain with him. Give him gentle reassurance, then ask him to walk forward again. Provided you remain confident and are patient, this will be transmitted to the horse and he will allow himself to be loaded without problem.

There are several reasons why a horse may refuse to enter a vehicle. It may be that he has previously been frightened, may be generally lacking in confidence, or he may merely be stubborn.

There are many ways to encourage a reluctant horse to load, but it is up to the handler to decide which method is the most suitable.

1. Horses are herd animals, so by putting a seasoned traveller in the box first, the reluctant animal will be more likely to follow.
2. If there is a front or a side ramp, it may be a help to lower it, as daylight shining through will make the horse feel less claustrophobic; this should also make him feel happier about walking forward and up the ramp.
3. Try lowering the angle of the ramp by backing the vehicle up a slope.
4. Ask a helper to stand behind the horse with a whip, making

sure they are at a safe distance to avoid being kicked. A sharp tap can work wonders.

5. Try fitting a rope to each side of the ramp. You will need two extra handlers and each one will need to hold a rope each. As the horse is led forward the handlers with the ropes must exchange places which will have the effect of driving the horse up the ramp. The ropes must be kept taut and, if necessary, pressure can be applied around the lower hindquarters of the horse.

6. Always be patient and allow plenty of time. If you appear at all anxious, the horse will surely know and as a consequence will become anxious himself.

7. If you find that your horse is strong to lead in a headcollar, lead him from a snaffle bridle placed over the headcollar. Once loaded and safely tied up, the bridle can be removed to allow the horse to travel in comfort.

When travelling, horses are happiest when they can feed from a securely tied haynet. Make sure that the vehicle is driven slowly and steadily; great care must be taken when accelerating, slowing down, and negotiating corners and uneven surfaces.

UNLOADING

Make sure all partitions are well secured and out of the way before even attempting to lead a horse down a ramp. Lead the horse steadily down the centre, allowing him time to judge his step. If you have a trailer, untie the horse or horses first before lifting the front bars.

GENERAL MAINTENANCE OF TRAILER OR HORSEBOX

- After each journey, all bedding should be removed and the box thoroughly mucked out; the floorboards should be allowed to completely dry out.

- Regularly check fuel and water.

- If towing, check towing-hitch for safety and that it is at the correct height.

- Check brakes, lights, indicators, and tyres for wear and correct pressure.

- Check that the vehicle is generally roadworthy.

- Occasionally, check floor of horsebox and fixtures and fittings for soundness.

AIR TRAVEL

This used to be a rarity. However, it has become increasingly common for horses to be transported by air. Most adapt easily, the same way they get used to travelling by road. Provided that the compartment on the aircraft is wide enough and that there is supervision by a competent handler, the journey should proceed without incident.

Before departure, contact a professional company which will advise you on cost, protection while travelling, feeding and health requirements.

When attending a show, it is a good idea to bring along an experienced friend to help with the horse and offer moral support.

Chapter Sixteen
PREPARING FOR A SHOW

Getting both horse and rider ready for a show is hard work and requires organization and skill. With practice, anyone can plait manes and tails and groom a horse to a high standard; moreover, the whole procedure can be most enjoyable.

It is assumed that, before competing, you will have already worked hard on your jumping, dressage or whatever equestrian discipline you have chosen. Now that the eve of the great day has arrived, it is time for meticulous preparation.

THE HORSE AND RIDER
Before the show, make sure you have all the clothing and equipment necessary for your chosen event. Everything should be spotlessly clean and in good order.

FOR SHOWING
The Rider
Hard hat
Jacket
Gloves
Long boots
Cane
Shirt and tie
Jodhpurs
Hairnet, if needed

The Horse
APPROPRIATE SADDLE
Dressage/Showing saddle for non-jumping classes or jumping or General-Purpose for working hunter. Double Bridle where appropriate.

BELOW: Horse and rider are equipped for a Working Hunter class. For this, the rider should wear mainly natural colours, and the horse plain leather tack.

OPPOSITE: For the Riding Horse class, both horse and rider can be rather more colourful.

BELOW: This horse has been provided with suitable tack and protective gear for a showjumping competition. The rider is also correctly dressed, with both horse and rider looking rather more colourful for the event.

LEFT: This pair are successfully competing at a local show, and both are looking very much the part.

FOR SHOWJUMPING

The Rider

Hard hat

Jacket

Back protector

Gloves

Long boots

Whip

Shirt and tie or stock

Jodhpurs

Hairnet, if needed

The Horse

Snaffle bridle or any other suitable bridle for jumping. Jumping/GP saddle, martingale with or without breastplate, protective leg wear, brushing or tendon boots and overreach boots.

FOR CROSS-COUNTRY

The Rider

Skull cap

Body protector

Coloured cross-country shirt

Gloves

Long boots

Whip

Jodhpurs

Hairnet, if needed

The Horse

Snaffle or more severe bridle.
Jumping/GP saddle with overgirth.
Martingale with breastplate,
overgirth and protective leg wear,
brushing, tendon boots or exercise
bandages and overreach boots.

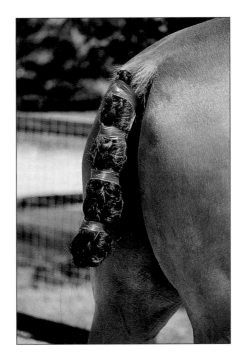

LEFT: The tail can be bound up in this way to protect it from becoming muddy in wet conditions

BELOW: Horse and rider are correctly dressed for a cross-country competition. Note that the rider is wearing a body protector under her shirt.

OPPOSITE: This action shot shows both horse and rider in performance and wearing the correct gear.

FOR DRESSAGE

The Rider

Hard hat

Shirt and tie or stock

Jacket

Gloves

Long boots

Dressage whip

Jodhpurs

Hairnet, if needed

The Horse

Preferably a dressage saddle, but a GP will do, with snaffle bridle for lower level, double for higher. No protective boots allowed.

ABOVE: In correct attire for a dressage competition.

RIGHT: In dressage, both horse and rider should appear as the epitome of elegance and harmony.

214

TACK AND EQUIPMENT

Make sure all tack, boots and other equipment is clean and ready. Remember that different disciplines require different gear, so be prepared. Take with you water buckets and a container of water, an anti-sweat rug, a day rug, and some concentrated feed and hay if you are to be out all day. Don't forget first-aid kits for both horse and rider. Relevant telephone numbers and a mobile telephone are also useful in case of emergency. The more preparation you do in advance, the easier the actual day will be.

Confirm details of your show entry times and that you have the necessary dressage test sheets, if required.

PREPARING THE HORSE

Plaiting the Mane This dramatically improves a horse's appearance, accentuating the head and neck and adding elegance and refinement. Always plait on the morning of the show; doing it the night before is unsatisfactory as the horse will probably disturb the plaits and they will get covered in dust.

Tools required are a mane comb, thread in the same colour as the horse's mane, a fairly large, blunt-ended needle, a water brush and scissors.

1. Make sure the mane has been thoroughly brushed and all knots removed. Dampen it down and divide it into an even number of equal sections along the neck and including the forelock. These can be temporarily secured with elastic bands.
2. Start behind the ears, leaving the forelock until last. Take the

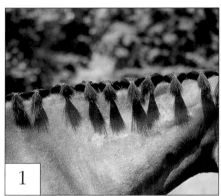

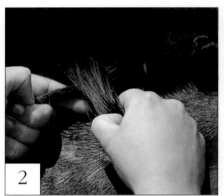

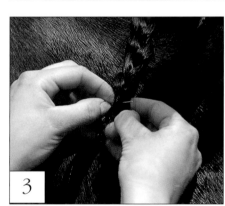

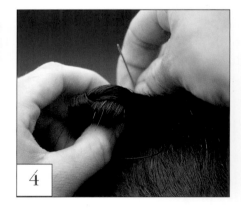

first section and plait/braid it right to the very end. Using the needle and plaiting thread, sew the end securely.
3. Turn the end of the plait under and sew it in to neaten the edges.
4. Roll the plait under until it forms a small, neat bobble. Make sure that it is nice and

tight. Sew it all together, trying not to let too much thread show. Finally, carefully trim away the excess thread.

TOP: A well plaited mane shows off the horse's neck to best advantage.

OPPOSITE: A plaited tail will accentuate the horse's tail carriage.

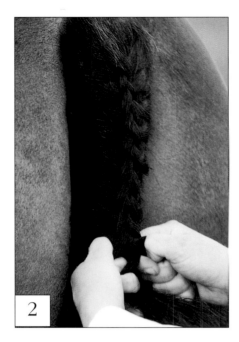

Plaiting the Tail This is a way of displaying the horse's hindquarters as well as giving the tail an attractive appearance. Like the mane, do not attempt this the day before as your work will probably not last the night and be spoiled.

1. After thoroughly brushing and combing the tail, incorporate small sections of tail hair from either side, starting at the top next to the dock to form a central plait. Continue down the tail, making sure the plait is neat and even.

2. When you reach the end of the dock, carry on plaiting the top section only until you reach the end. Turn the plait under and sew it in to hide the end. To keep the plait in place and to protect the tail when travelling, apply a tail bandage; when removing it, take care not to destroy the plait in the process.

For the show, a horse will require a really thorough grooming, which will include washing the mane and tail (see page 160). Afterwards, put a day rug on or, if the weather is hot, use a summer sheet to keep the horse clean.

OVERLEAF: These two have just arrived at a show and are anticipating a good day ahead.

Chapter Seventeen
TRAINING YOUR HORSE

Schooling/training in the manège or on a flat, soft area of ground will improve a horse's balance, strength, fitness and obedience and make him a pleasure to ride.

A horse that is an experienced schoolmaster will be able to help his rider through the various points of dressage, along with an instructor to assist. For those with a less experienced or young horse, it will be the rider's task to train the horse. All riders contemplating dressage or flat work must engage a good instructor, as bad habits can easily develop without regular tuition. Choose an instructor suitable to your requirements. For instance, if you are very inexperienced and need to work on the basics, it is a waste of money to pay for a expensive and fashionable trainer who competes in Grand Prix dressage. When selecting an instructor, a good guideline is to check out their qualifications and general reputation; finally it is important that you get on well together, as a

BELOW: Practising dressage movements in the manège will improve the horse's balance and fitness.

OPPOSITE: This young rider is working her horse in walk.

clash of personalities is the last thing you need.

It is important that you try to understand your horse. Be aware that he is a sensitive and generous animal, qualities which must

never be abused. When some aspect is difficult to achieve, don't blame the horse, first blame yourself and try not to let your own mood swings upset him. A heavy-handed, angry approach will always fail.

Nearly all horses are capable of working well on the flat. This is because all the dressage movements are ones that horses perform every day while playing and relaxing in the paddock. It is such a pleasure to see a horse performing *passages* in front of his companions when at play; all that is happening in the manège

is that you are asking him to perform those movements on command.

Much can be done to improve your overall performance when you are not riding. Reading, attending lectures, demonstrations and competitions will all improve your riding skills, as well as helping you to identify your goals and aims.

POSITION OF THE RIDER

It is most important that you sit correctly, as a balanced rider seated in the correct position will be a positive help to a horse

when executing his movements.

Aim to sit tall in the deepest part of the saddle, legs stretched loosely downwards, and the heels pressed down. The upper arms should be relaxed with the elbows gently flexed and the wrists softly rounded. Fingers should be closed with thumbs on top. The elbows and wrists should trace a straight, imaginary line to the bit.

Achieving a good position takes time and practice, but there are some excellent ways to help you do this. Stretching, as a warm-up exercise is one of these.

Riding without stirrups will

help improve the seat and balance. This should be done regularly for short periods. Lunge lessons without stirrups are also beneficial, enabling you to concentrate on your position without having to worry about controlling the horse.

THE NATURAL AIDS

These are signals given to the horse to ask him to go forward, sideways, stop, turn, etc. Our own natural aids are our legs, seat, weight, hands and voice.

The legs should hang loosely but remain very close to the horse's side. The aid or leg signal should be given as lightly as possible. Refrain from continuous kicking which will eventually deaden the horse's reaction, ending in a vicious circle of disobedience.

The seat and weight has a great influence on the horse's way of going. The rider should sit as deeply as possible and go with the horse's every movement. Good control of the seat will enable the rider to slow the horse down or shorten or lengthen his steps. Remember your posture at all times; do not allow yourself to lean too far forward or back.

The rein aids have to be applied as lightly as possible, as any rough or clumsy movement will cause pain to the horse. While the hands should be kept as still as possible, they must still maintain an elastic contact with the horse's mouth.

The voice is a useful aid to reassure a horse or reward him. Horses have very good hearing so there is no need to shout. In a dressage test, however, use of the voice is not permitted. If the

judge hears you talking to your horse you will be penalized.

ARTIFICIAL AIDS

The whip should only be used to reinforce the leg aid, not to punish. Once you realize your horse has decided to ignore your light leg aid, one quick tap of a schooling whip should wake him up. Should he surge forward as a

result of the tap, you must be very careful not to catch him in the mouth.

ABOVE: Training in the open can be beneficial as the rider will have to work harder to keep the horse between leg and hand.

OPPOSITE: Correct position of the rider.

This horse is being ridden in canter, which is the most difficult pace to perform. It require a good deal of balance and impulsion.

Spurs should only be used by experienced riders who can fully control their leg position. They are used to refine and aid movement rather than punish. Spurs should always be blunt and angled straight or downwards.

THE CORRECT WAY OF GOING

A horse going correctly is a pleasure to watch, with every movement appearing fluid and effortless. The horse should be completely relaxed but still feel powerful. His outline will become more rounded and his jaw and poll relaxed. Ideally, he will carry his head just in front of the vertical. Power will originate in the hindquarters which will be carried through the back to the bit. The way of going is known as 'on the bit'.

When a horse is on the bit it is very vulnerable; it is vitally important, therefore, that your hands move in harmony with the horse's mouth. The weight in your hands should be as even as possible and should be maintained through all the paces. This feeling is known as 'the contact'.

THE PACES

The Walk A correct walk should be relaxed, rhythmic, energetic but unhurried. It should have four clear beats. The sequence of steps is near-fore, off-hind, off-fore, near-hind.

A free walk gives the horse an opportunity to stretch and relax. He should be allowed to take the rein forward and down.

In a medium walk, he should be on the bit, with medium-length elastic steps and should over-track.

When making a transition from free to medium walk, or vice-versa, be sure the aids are given smoothly, thus maintaining rhythm and straightness.

The Trot This is a two-time pace. It should be rhythmical and active. Most riders will find the rising trot more comfortable than the sitting trot, where the rider has to absorb all the movement. However, with practice, the rider will become accustomed to both. Do not attempt prolonged periods of sitting trot on young or inexperienced horses, as this could be injurious.

Once the working trot has been perfected, the rider can begin to ask for some lengthened strides in trot. The horse must be asked to cover more ground without quickening the pace. First establish a good steady trot, then use a slightly stronger leg aid to

BELOW: The walk is a four-time pace. A good walk should have rhythm and balance and care should be taken that the rider does not push the horse forward out of his stride.

RIGHT: This elegant horse is performing a good working trot in a dressage competition.

encourage the horse to step further forward so that he can lengthen his body. With practice, the horse will enthusiastically respond as you release the contained energy you have created.

The Canter This pace has three beats. It should be flowing and springy and have a clear moment of suspension. When riding in canter, the horse will seem light on his feet if he is going correctly.

As canter is a faster pace than trot, it will require more balance; before asking for canter, therefore, make sure you have the best possible quality of trot. Ask for

canter in a corner or on a large circle. In this way you can be sure the horse will strike off on the correct lead. Keep a steady contact on the outside rein with a more passive inside rein to maintain the bend. Place the inside leg on the girth, then

BELOW: During lengthened strides, the horse must cover more ground, but without quickening the trot.

OPPOSITE: Initially, practise sitting trot for short periods of time; this can be progressively built up as the fitness and balance of both horse and rider increases.

nudge the horse, the outside leg slightly further back behind the girth. The horse should then strike off correctly. Once cantering, go with the horse's movement and be careful to retain your balance. Do not be tempted to look down.

THE SCHOOLING SESSION

It is a good idea to time this so that you can gradually build up the length of time spent in the school. When a horse is unfit, it may be that around 20 minutes will suffice, but in time the session can be built up to from about 3/4 of a hour to one hour.

If the horse is going exceptionally well, you may wish to cut the session short in order to end on a good note.

Make sure that you give the horse frequent breaks in walk throughout the session.

Always begin the schooling session with about 10 minutes in walk. Walk the horse on a fairly loose rein. This will give you both time to loosen and warm up.

Begin the trot also on a loose rein so that the horse can stretch and establish his own balance. Once he is warm you can start to shorten the reins gradually and ask the horse to work on the bit. Large circles, turns and serpentines will help to engage the hindquarters and improve balance. Make sure that you ride

OPPOSITE: Practise canter initially along straight lines and enlarged circles. As the canter improves, more difficult movements can be attempted.

OVERLEAF: A well schooled horse is a lasting pleasure.

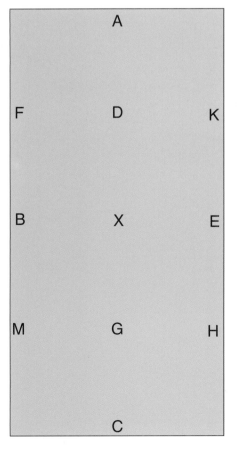

evenly on both reins and that you concentrate on delivering the lightest possible aids; throughout this, sit up straight and concentrate on the job in hand. Practise upward and downward transitions between walk and trot so that you do not stay in the same pace for too long. Try to get the transitions as smooth as possible and concentrate on accurate circles and other movements.

Towards the end of the session, you can introduce canter on either rein. As canter is a strenuous activity for a horse, make sure it is not overdone.

The more experienced rider can now begin to introduce some lateral work. This will increase the horse's manoeuvrability and loosen his movements. Leg-

yielding, turn-on-the-forehand and shoulder-in are all movements which can be learned fairly easily.

Finish up the session with some work on a longer rein to allow the horse to stretch; finally, walk for a few minutes on a loose rein, allowing the horse to cool down before putting him away.

ABOVE: The horse should stand perfectly still when halted. Make sure that you practise this regularly.

LEFT: A short dressage arena.

OPPOSITE: This horse is working in a relaxed manner in trot.

JUMPING

Jumping should be fun for horse and rider and is most rewarding when everything goes according to plan.

When schooling a young horse over jumps, start with a height that suits you both.

The rider's position and balance is very important: there must be a very secure lower leg and the ability to 'fold' over the fence. The rider's stirrup length should be a least two holes shorter than for everyday riding.

BELOW: The correct jumping position.

BOTTOM: Work over trotting poles is good for improving balance.

RIGHT: Grids will help improve athleticism.

OVERLEAF: Schooling your horse at home will pay off in the showjumping arena.

Between fences, the body should be inclined slightly forward with the thighs and hips resting lightly in the saddle. The heels should be pressed downwards.

When approaching a jump, the rider must maintain the horse's rhythm, balance and impulsion. A light consistent contact on the reins and a steady lower leg resting on the horse's sides will instil confidence. Always approach the jump from the straightest angle possible. Just before the moment of take-off, the horse will lower his head; he will take a good look at the fence and measure the height. On take-off, the well positioned rider should 'fold' naturally and hands, while maintaining a light contact, must allow forwards to give the horse full freedom of his head and neck. Occasionally the rider will get 'left behind' (this happens to the best riders). When this happens, the rider must learn from the experience and be prepared to 'slip the reins' through his fingers, allowing the horse freedom.

For novice riders and for horses just learning to jump, it is a good idea to fit the horse with a neck strap. This way, if you feel in danger of getting left behind on the approach, you can hold onto it with a couple of fingers which will help to avoid pulling the horse unnecessarily in the mouth.

Be careful not to do too much in one session: jumping is strenuous for the horse and once tired he will begin to lose enthusiasm. Remember to finish on a good note when you both still have plenty of energy left.

A clever, agile horse will get itself out of trouble.

Chapter Eighteen
GOING OUT FOR A RIDE

Riding in the open countryside is a wonderful experience and both horse and rider will enjoy the experience equally. Most horses are more enthusiastic when away from the manège as it gives them a chance to unwind from the rigors of training. Hacking out is great for improving fitness.

It is important that you are properly dressed. Make sure you wear a hard hat, secured with a chin strap, sensible boots, adequately warm clothing and, if you ride on the road, a fluorescent tabard. In fact, it cannot be overestimated how essential it is to make yourself as conspicuous as possible to other road users. Unfortunately, there are too many accidents involving horses on our roads today, so the

BELOW: If you are able to ride away from busy roads, you will be able to exercise your dog at the same time as your horse.

OPPOSITE: Going out for a ride with a friend is a great way to spend an afternoon.

OVERLEAF: Riding in Australia.

best advice is to avoid them if at all possible. If you have to ride on the road it is safest to ride in single file, but occasionally two abreast is the safest option, e.g. when a young, or nervous horse requires shielding from the traffic, or a novice rider needs a barrier between himself and the traffic.

When riding out, it is best as part of a group, when if anything untoward should occur, you will have someone else to turn to. Whether in company or not, you should always acquaint someone with the route you are intending to take.

After giving the horse a warm-up in walk for about 10 minutes, the paces can be varied throughout the ride, with the terrain usually indicating the pace.

Where the ground is waterlogged, rutted or stony, it will be best to walk. However, where the ground is good and the surroundings suitable, a trot and canter may be appropriate. Whatever pace you choose, make sure you maintain control over the horse and try to keep him working forward and in good rhythm throughout the ride.

RIGHT: Only ride on the road when you are confident that your horse is good in traffic and make sure that you are both highly visible.

OPPOSITE: When riding out, follow approved trails and tracks; only ride on private land with the permission of the owner.

POINTS OF THE HORSE

KEY

1 Poll
2 Forehead
3 Nostril
4 Muzzle
5 Chin groove
6 Jowl
7 Angle of jaw
8 Windpipe
9 Jugular groove
10 Point of shoulder
11 Shoulder
12 Breast
13 Forearm
14 Knee
15 Cannon bone
16 Fetlock
17 Coronet
18 Hoof
19 Pastern
20 Bulb of heel
21 Ergot
22 Point of elbow
23 Ribs
24 Belly
25 Sheath (male)
26 Stifle
27 Hock
28 Gaskin
29 Thigh
30 Flank
31 Hindquarters
32 Dock
33 Croup
34 Loins
35 Back
36 Withers
37 Crest
38 Neck

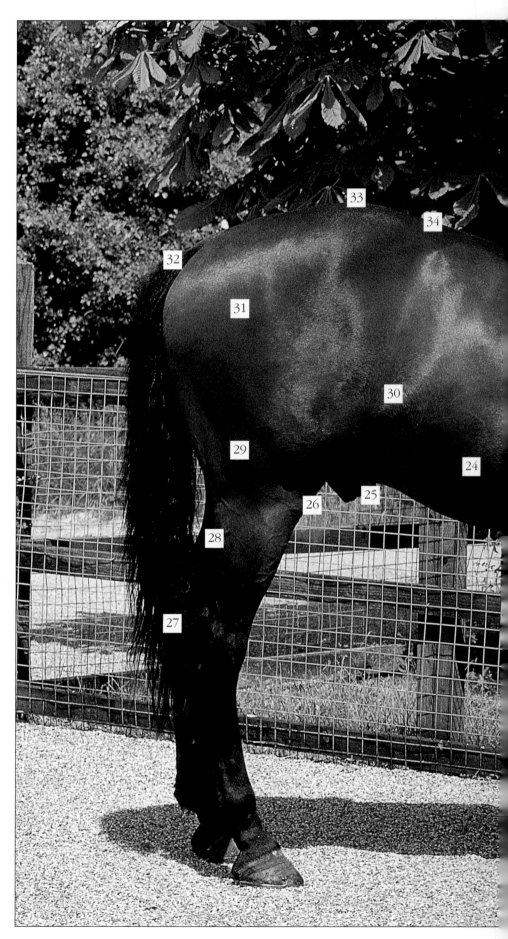

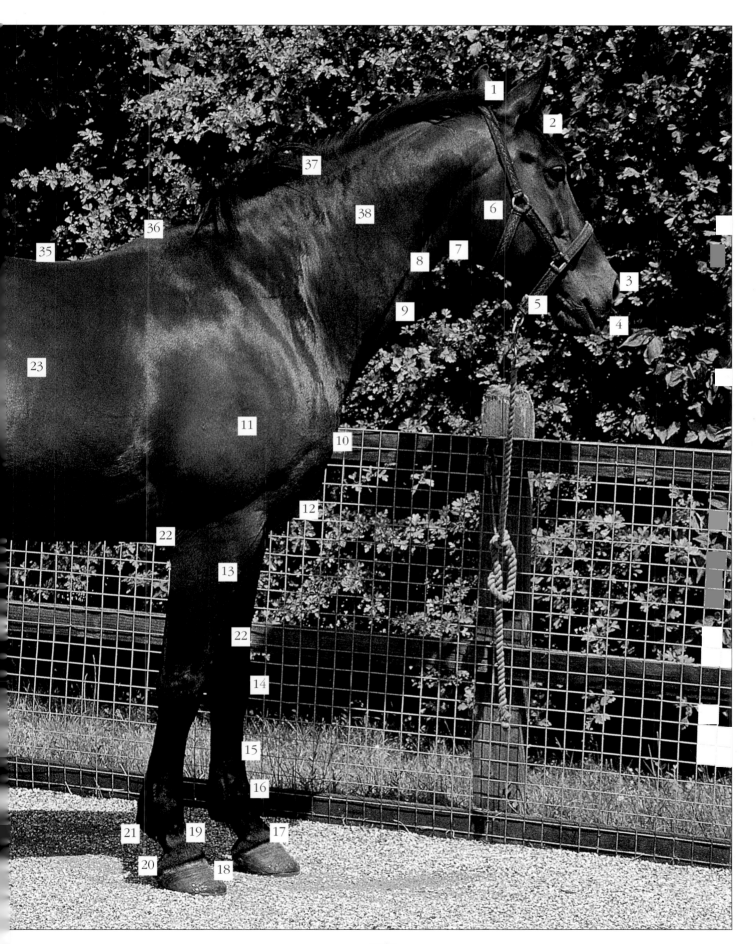

Action The way in which a horse moves.

Aids Recognized signals used by the rider to pass instructions to the horse. *Natural aids* are conveyed through the legs, hands, body and voice and *artificial aids* include whips, spurs and other items such as martingales.

At Grass A horse which either lives in a field all year round or which is turned out from time to time.

Bad Doer (Unthrifty Horse) A horse that fails to thrive, even when fed the requisite amounts of food.

Bit The mouthpiece fitted to a bridle used to aid the rider's control of the horse. There are many different kinds such as the snaffle.

'Bone' A term used in conformation which refers to the circumference below the knee. If this is generous the horse is described as having 'plenty of bone', if not, it is said to be 'short of bone'.

Box, to To lead a horse up a ramp and into a horsebox, van or trailer.

Brushing (Interfering) When the inside of the horse's hind or foreleg is struck by the opposite leg. Brushing boots can be used as a protection against this.

Cavesson Either a simple noseband or a lunging cavesson used for breaking and schooling horses on a lunge-rein.

Chaff Finely chopped hay used to add bulk to the feed or to prevent the horse from bolting his food.

Cold Hosing Using a stream of cold water to reduce inflammation.

Concussion The jarring caused to the feet and legs of a horse when working on hard ground.

Double Bridle Through the use of a bridle with two bits, the snaffle and the curb, the rider can exercise a greater degree of control over his mount than he would if he used an ordinary bridle.

Dressage The training of the horse to perform in a classical tradition. The aim is to achieve obedience, control and suppleness.

Eventing A competition involving the three disciplines of dressage, cross-country and showjumping.

Frog The V-shaped part of the horse's foot which acts as a shock absorber.

Gamgee Gauze-covered cotton-wool used with bandages or leg wraps, or to give extra support or protection to a horse's legs.

Going, the (Footing) The condition of the ground.

Good Doer (Easy Keeper) A horse which remains in good condition whatever the circumstances.

Hack A term used for going out for a ride. Also a type of horse.

Hand A unit of 4 inches (10cm) used to measure the height of a horse.

Hunter A type of horse of any breed suitable for the hunting field.

Leading-Rein (Lead Shank) Long rope attached to the bit by which the horse can be led.

Lunge, to Training a horse on a long rein attached to a cavesson, when the trainer uses a lunge whip to encourage the horse

Manège An arena or school which has been marked out in the traditional method. Used for schooling horses and for teaching people to ride.

Martingale An item of tack used to give the rider a greater degree of control over a horse.

Nearside The left-hand side of a horse.

Offside The right-hand side of a horse.

Points of the Horse Terms and names given to the various parts of the horse's exterior anatomy.

Pull, to The process of tidying or thinning the mane and tail.

Quartering A quick grooming before exercise.

School An area marked out in a traditional way where horses are trained and exercised.

Side-reins Used to steady the horse and improve his outline. One end of the rein is fixed to the bit and the other to either the front of the saddle or a roller.

Snaffle Bit A type of simple mouthpiece of which there are many different kinds.

Spurs An artificial aid or device fitted to the rider's boot to encourage the horse forward.

Strike-off The first step of the canter.

Surcingle or Overgirth A strap, usually of webbing, which passes over the horse's back and under his belly and is used to secure a rug or saddle.

Tack A collective term used for describing items of saddlery.

Thoroughbred Dating from the 17th century, this is probably one of the most famous breeds of horse.

Trailer A form of transportation for horses which is towed behind another vehicle.

Turn-Out To put a horse out in a field.

Twitch A device used to restrain a nervous or impetuous horse, it should only be used by an expert.

Vice Any bad habit a horse may develop and which may render it unsound.

Wind A horse's respiration when working.

INDEX